WAKING UP SAD
A Diary of Unrequited Loves

Insung Hwang

BROWN ACORN PRESS

ISBN: 978-0-9848343-2-7
©2012 Insung Hwang

www.brownacorn.com

Contents

Introduction

Professional "liars" such as politicians and magicians always know the truth. If they didn't, they wouldn't know what to *hide* and what to *reveal*. Professionals have a clear understanding of who they are and whom they are fooling. On the other hand, amateurs don't always know who the liar is and who the fool is. Sometimes we confuse the two. Oftentimes, it's one and the same. Sometimes in an effort to find the truth, we catch ourselves telling this lie. When we do, we change direction in order to find the *real* truth. We keep repeating this until we either give up or get up and try again.

This *process of failure* is known as *waking up*. This book is a 22-year documentation of that process.

There are passages in my diary that make me cringe. "Did I really write *this*? How can this be the same person who wrote *that*?" These are questions I asked myself as I assessed whether this book might be useful for someone else to read. When the answer was still "yes" I decided to publish it.

If you are someone like me who tend to have a little melancholy in your genes and a natural curiosity for the nature of love and reality, you might find it useful in reading the text—not always as words of wisdom, but in fact as words of ignorance muttered, as only they can be, through pain and suffering.

The names of the people have been changed in case anyone gets really mad at me. Items in [brackets] are notes that I have entered for clarity. They are not part of the original hand-written journals. Also, I am not a believer in *obligatory* daily journal writing. I really don't have that much to say *every* day. However, I do believe in writing *anytime* and *every time* an interesting thought or feeling comes over me. So, some entries will have a lapse in time, as much as many months or even years while other lapses are hours, or even minutes.

1989 Aware in my Sleep

OCTOBER 2, 1989

<u>I</u> THINK SO.

I <u>THINK</u> SO.

I THINK <u>SO.</u>

OCTOBER 7, 1989

Do I feel because I think?

Or

Do I think because I feel?

4:35 pm – I feel sad (a little). Oh, I met with Pastor Michael at church. He'll be calling me sometime this week to get together. I wish I had someone to talk to or just be with.

I'm in need of company. I feel afraid to write in here everything I feel or think because it may be read by someone(s) I don't want to open myself to. I'm 23 years old now. I'm still a very closed person. I can't share myself, my feelings with just anyone. Maybe it's because I have a hard time trusting people. One, I don't think people are *that* good. I know we can't all be like Jesus, but one would think there should be some sincere, honest people. I've been hurt many times, situations where I trust somebody really believing in what they say, only to be a deception.

Trust is a very interesting thing. No one wants to be the first to put forth his hand, afraid that the other may bite it. Unfortunately, there will be <u>no</u> trust if no one puts out her hand. I feel my hands and fingers are getting shorter from being bit. Eventually, I may not have a hand to put forth. That is, I may not trust anyone, any longer. I hope that won't be the case. I know that's not the case with God. I wonder how many people I have hurt?

OCTOBER 29, 1989

[I had a habit of drawing the places I lived in]

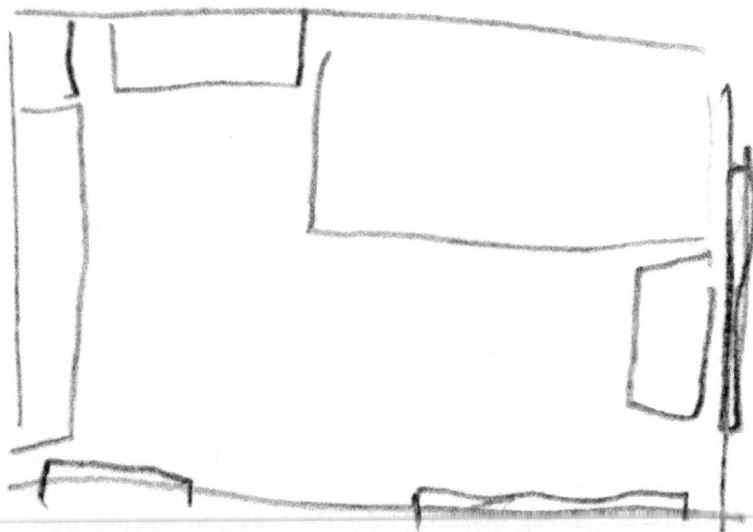

OCTOBER 19, 1989

I'm so lost. I try not to conform to anything–not race, not sex, not anything. Maybe in not conforming to anything, I am without "identity." I don't want to conform to anything because I'm afraid of losing myself —as an individual. I joined PCF [Poly Christian Fellowship] last year and at times I felt I was lost (losing myself in the group). Is this called selfishness? In The Bible, we are told to lose ourselves for others. I don't get it!! I don't understand. I'm so very lonely. I feel like there's no one to talk to (and have them understand). Even God seems so far away. I wish I had a pet. But I guess it would only remind me of my loneliness. I can't seem to find life worthwhile, right now anyway. *How* did I know I was going to be born? I guess the point is, if you have a good life, you are thankful you got the gift of life. If you have a bad life, you ask why you were born—you were never asked to be born. *Everything*, even truth seems to be a matter of perception. That's too bad.

I've been feeling guilty lately, not because I'm not reacting to situations in a positive way—But because, I *don't* feel guilty. My mother told me that she may be moving to New York. And I felt somewhat relieved inside, like a burden coming off my chest. I guess I'm supposed to feel sad because she's moving away, but I don't. I feel guilty because I don't feel sad. I feel as alive as a brick.

THINGS I LIKE:

- Pizza
- Tea
- Riding my bike
- My family
- Potatoes
- Alex
- Mary
- My cousin Nina
- My sisters and brotherst
- Sports cars
- Making new friends
- Money
- Sex (with the right person)
- Clothes
- Flowers

THINGS I DON'T LIKE:

- Losing old friends
- Losing new friends
- Losing
- Money!
- Sex (with the wrong person)
- Boredom

NOVEMBER 19, 1989

(P.M.)

Well, Ann wasn't in front of the U.U. [University Union] like we had planned. I was really upset at first, but now I don't really care. I really don't care about anything. I guess I could care, but I don't think I really want to. Nothing seems to matter. No matter what happens to my life, life itself still goes on. Trees still grow. The wind still blows. I don't quite understand myself. I am the most complicated person I ever knew. There are parts of me that show up that I never knew existed. I don't understand why I write all this. Let me try to guess. (1) It could be because I don't have anyone to talk to about it with. (2) Because I can't open up. (3) I'm afraid to open up. Or (4) I want to get out my frustrations.

Who cares?

I think because I'm so bored; because I can't seem to get the "point" in life; because I'm lonely; whatever, I've been lately wanting to make a lot of money—lots of it. That's all I want right now. God seems so far away. Everything seems so far away. I feel like my life is a dream I had once long ago. 23 years of it, and what do I have to show for it? All I have is a vague image of ideas. That's all. Ideas like hate, love, deceit, pain, pleasure, fear. I guess I still have hope. But what the fuck does that mean?! Hope for what?! Nothing lasts forever. I mean, take a look at a worm: It gets eaten by birds. And birds get eaten by other animals, including people. Pretty soon my life will be over. I die. I turn into dust, into dirt to become food for the worms. I don't' understand any of it!

Then why does it *seem* to matter when we are hurt or loved or cheated? It would seem to me that there must be a reason for our reasoning/questioning. But there's no way of knowing. Some people *choose* to believe that there is nothing more after this life. And they choose to live their lives that way. Some people *choose* to believe that there is something after this life. They call it eternal life. I cannot possibly imagine living forever, in pure pain (hell) or pure joy (heaven). In order to have life there must be death and birth—birth at the beginning and death at the end. However in eternal life (heaven or hell), there is no beginning and there is no end. Thus, there is no eternal life.

I choose not to believe either one of them because I really don't know for sure. And I will not (cannot) believe what I don't understand. How can anyone?

Strange thing is, in order to understand something, there must be some standard or something neutral or something we know to be *true* in the first place to compare our understanding to. But how do we know what's true? In order to have truth, there must also be a beginning and an end. There is only one truth I am pretty sure of. I was born and I will die. This gives me the basis for comparison of truth and understanding. The afterlife (and before-life) is something I am not so sure of. I guess what I am saying is, I want to have, I guess, lots of money to spend. I mean if I am basing truth and understanding by my life and death, then what is there to do on this planet but to buy a big house, nice cars, screw lots of women, and go jumping out of airplanes?

Well then, what about love? I don't understand it so how can I believe such a thing exists? This is not to say, if I don't know how an airplane works (or any other kind of concept or idea) I don't believe it exists. What I think I mean is this: I guess there is a possibility of love, but I won't pretend that I understand. In comparison to God: We create the word "love" and the word "God" but the actual concepts come from unknown sources. We can say God created them, or we can say we created them. Both statements would seem valid with the correct reasoning. I have heard enough to see that both sides are possible. The idea of God creating us seems self-explanatory. But *we* creating God may not be so simple. What came first, the chicken or the egg? Did Adam have a belly button? Because God is not tangible, God is more of a concept than anything else—to explain (or at least try to explain) why we are here on this planet. So, did we create God? Or did God create us? If God created us, then who created God? How can God just exist? In order *just* exist, this would mean he would not have a purpose. Thus, we would not have a purpose. How can *anything* be sovereign? But if nothing is sovereign, it would be an endless cycle. Then this would be meaningless as well. That is, Jesus gave us life by his death. We give life to worms by our death.

Anyway, in order for something to *just* exist, one would have to be a rock or a planet or something of that nature. "Man does not live on bread alone." This is true because if we did, we would be out with the sheep grazing, rather than building racing cars and skyscrapers.

I better get some sleep. No matter how much I write, I won't be one step further.

One more: a person is born and a person will die, but he may never really *live.* I want to live!

Just one more: If man created love, I can understand it. But I won't like it. If God created love, then I won't understand it.

NOVEMBER 27, 1989

I think I'm *finally* accepting the fact that I am *truly* alone on Earth. You know, it's not so bad. I kind of like it.

I found two ingredients of life (the essential makeup, not the characteristics of it). Everything that is in existence has two properties: (1)

Means (2) End. Think about it.

I'm pretty bored.

Isn't it pretty interesting? I feel like I have only two real friends: God and me. It feels funny thinking this way because I'm "supposed" to have lots of friends and be happy if I have God as a friend. Well, I don't (have many friends, that is). It's hard to know what a friend is.

DECEMBER 6, 1989

There is no such thing as a compliment. If there is, then it would be known as a lie. Never mind. I take that back. A compliment is defined as: a formal expression of esteem, respect, affection, or admiration.

Anyway, I just took my Philosophy of Art final. I'm done for the quarter! Feels good! I'm moving my stuff to Mel's this Saturday. I'm always moving, so it seems. I guess I'm growing and/or learning. With every change comes new experience. Life is made up of balances. Maybe my experiences outweigh my current residence. Therefore, it would be necessary to move in order to keep the balance. Everything is so well balanced in this world like pleasure/pain, high/low, good/bad, male/female, love/hate, heaven/hell, life/death, rich/poor, happy/sad.

For the longest time I couldn't understand happiness and satisfaction.

I think happiness is satisfaction *and* knowing why one is satisfied. I can't get happiness because I can't get satisfaction. I can't get satisfaction because I'm trying to get happiness. I have a right to happiness, but I won't get it if that's my sole motive. I think satisfaction may come from doing things right (not for my happiness but for the sake of goodness or righteousness)—doing right for mankind and not just for myself.

I'm a victim on the path of my own thinking, like painting a door then painting a "wet paint" sign, then painting a "wet paint" sign for the wet paint sign, then painting a "wet paint" sign for the wet paint sign for the wet paint sign. Am I the thinking killer whose victim is me? Or am I the victim whose thinking killer is me? Aaagh! In thinking the way I do, I have two perspectives: One, no matter how much thinking I do or how much I achieve mentally, life still goes on like it always has, i.e. trees still grow, wind still blows. Or two, what is real is *what* is in my mind. The trees and wind may or may not really exist, but I perceive them to be. In this case, lots of things have changed. After all, all we really have are ideas, thoughts, or memories, all of which are non-tangible. Life then is really not tangible as otherwise perceived. Reality only exists if we attach meaning to them. I see a flower vase in my room. I could just as well have imagined it. But because my mind says there is a flower vase (a meaning) in the room, I believe it. If my mind told me there's a horse in the room, I would believe it. Therefore, reality for example, is not an action but rather our reaction (perception) to the actions (or objects). Reality is not the flower vase. The flower vase becomes real when we think (believe) it is.

1990 Weird Dreams

JANUARY 3, 1990

What bothers me is that I'm not pure in any way. I don't mean innocence or goodness. But I feel like I'm not a "thoroughbred" in any way. I have no consistency. I'm made up of bits and pieces of everywhere, everyplace, and every person. I can't find a passion. That is what I mean by having no purity. The only thing that comes close to pure is my pain. Pain is the closest passion I have. Unfortunately, I can't make a living with pain. I know it's difficult to make a living out of any kind of passion (like music for example). But when a person's passion is lived through, success (reward) is present; the triumph; the glory. But how do I achieve success in pain?

JANUARY 4, 1990

I know so little about the current issues around me. Political issues for example. I feel like I'm so under-informed. At least I feel like I should know more. But I don't want to know more, really. I don't care. It's my careless attitude that bothers me. I suppose a person can be involved only to a certain extent, but somehow I feel inadequate. This is the side of me that is not quite developed yet, or my interest in it anyway.

I can't be honest with myself. It's so hard, but I keep telling myself lies. I think I'm trying too hard to be my own person, when all I have to do is nothing. I guess one doesn't *try* to do *nothing*; it just happens. I'm so wrapped up in my own world; in my own self. It's so hard to get out. Strange, for so many people, it's very hard to get in. I've seen enough of me for a while, for a long while. I want to see the rest of the world. But truthfully, I'm sort of scared. I've been living a very sheltered life, in a way. And I'm so afraid of being (being called) a failure. I don't want to fail in anything. I guess that's why I don't succeed. I guess that's why I don't have a passion. I have not failed enough in any one area—just a little here, just a little there. If I make enough errors in one area, I will surely succeed if I don't make all the same mistakes.

I'm beginning to understand my passion. A passion is a multitude of failure overcome by continual effort for success. And I'm trying so hard to overcome my failures. The results of failure include depression, terrible loneliness, poor self-esteem, etc.

JANUARY 7, 1990

What is <u>a</u> love? A love would be music. A love would be racing cars. A love would be your wife. A love would be art. But what <u>is</u> love? It may contain passion. No, it <u>does</u> contain passion. Love definitely contains passion. If I say I love music (as a musician) I must have failed many times to produce the desired result. But the *continual effort* for success is always there (passion). It also includes some form of "communication" between the love-er and the love-ee—like learning to play an instrument and finally playing something right. In this case the love-ee is the music; the "communicator" is the musical instrument; the love-er is the musician. In a human relationship, like at Christmas time, the gift would be the "communicator" between the love-er (giver) and the love-ee (receiver). In this case, the gift, although material in nature, is actually the communicative device for the true "communicator"; a compliment, adoration, admiration, or the like. There are certainly other "communicators" I have not mentioned, like sex. Still, sex would only be a communicative device for the true "communicator" like kindness and affection and sincerity. Love includes a decision. A love-er

[…Stopped writing]

(NIGHT)

I think in 1985 I defined Passion as "a raging appetite of emotions." Now, January 1990, Passion is "a multitude of failures overcome by continual effort for success."

JANUARY 10, 1990

11:56 PM. I'm beginning to feel free-er.

JANUARY 20, 1990

Yes, I was feeling free, but I think the drawing should have looked like this:

With freedom comes responsibility to handle that power. Yes, freedom is power. And yes I feel free. I am so free that I have thoughts of rape (or the like), the limits of my mind. These really don't seem to be a limit. It is so big and vast. I could wander for quite a long time in my mind/freedom. I am so incredibly free. But this thinking is like that of Mr. Hyde (of Jekyll & Hyde). How far can I go? How free am I? Am I so free that I may continue with my thoughts of hurting other people or even myself? Am I so free I can even choose to enjoy pain and anger? There must be a God. (There better be a God!)

I wish I could talk to somebody. But the people I know seem to be on one side of the fence or the other. I am trapped in between. They either seem to be on the good side and wonder how weird or sick I can be. Or on the bad side (the not-so-good) side and wonder why I am such a religious freak. I am so lonely. Worse, I feel like a hypocrite, although I am not lying to myself. Isn't there somebody who knows Christ and also know about the possibilities of the mind? I am sad.

JANUARY 21, 1990

What I find so interesting is that no matter what happens, days go by constantly. It doesn't matter if someone dies. It doesn't matter who the president of the United States is. It doesn't matter if someone has a bad day or good day. It doesn't matter if the whales are migrating to a warmer spot. It doesn't matter if Coke is better than Pepsi. It doesn't matter if people hate you. It doesn't matter if they like you either. It doesn't matter if I have a lot of money. It doesn't matter if I care. It doesn't matter if I don't care. It doesn't matter if I fail a class. It doesn't matter if live. The trees still grow. The birds still fly.

My mind is wandering. I'm tired. It's exactly 12:00 midnight.

You know, I used to have this idea of the type of person I'd like to meet. She used to be very interesting all sorts of ways. You know, very sophisticated, etc., etc., etc. Well now I think I just want someone with a warm smile and a sincere heart. That's all.

FEBRUARY 13, 1990

Nothing exists without a purpose, however small.

Sometimes it's hard to see my own purpose.

FEBRUARY 15, 1990

Welcome. Why are you here?

Who knows? But you arrived by yourself. You certainly travel light. What? No luggage? No cargo? How will you eat. How will you sleep? Do you know anyone in this place?

Well, come. I'll show you what's available here. You'll have to choose however where to go. If you decide to stay here, you will find that they may give you all the things you didn't bring with you like food and money to buy clothes, etc. Or it may lead to worse than what you already have right now, nothing (but yourself). They'll strip away every part of you, rob you of your rights, rape you, and leave you to nothing.

What's that? You want to know how you can end up with the good stuff? How should I know? I just work here.

Now what do you want to know? That's my scar from a fight I was in about two years ago. Hey aren't you getting a little personal? Look, I realize this is the first time you're here. It can look a little frightening at first, but you'll get used to it (the fright that is). It won't be so bad. You'll have new friends. Everything will be just fine. I'll have to warn you. You get lonely at times, but you'll have friends that are lonely too.

What do you mean you were never asked to be here? What's the matter with you? You think somebody threw you into the plane and sent you here? Let's be reasonable. If you didn't come here by your will, then you must have been drugged or hit over the head. Somebody must have sent you.

FEBRUARY 23, 1990

(SATURDAY MORNING)

What a weird dream. There were all these birds everywhere hidden in these dry thorn-like bushes on small trees. I had turned on the sprinkler system (very high) to get rid of these birds (most were black). They started flying everywhere! They were trying to escape. I think some had died and fell to the ground. So, I tried to duck and not get hit by these birds and/or their droppings.

Next thing I knew there were some kind of battle going on. There were missiles and bullets flying everywhere. Brian [my brother] and I couldn't get into this yellow VW convertible to escape because the girl who was driving it said there was no room. But as she drove away I saw there was a whole empty back seat. In fact there were three rows of seats in this VW. There was a missile headed toward us. Brian and I jumped into a ditch. I made it. Brian got hit on his right arm. We were almost at the chain-link fence gate. But the Russians started attacking from the other side of the fence. So we jumped off the road, off the side of the hill, and into this dry, leafless tree. It must have been like a 30 to 50 foot jump. I'm surprised that the branches didn't skewer us.

(another part of the dream)

I was being chased by some police or authorities. In this dream I was an illegal Mexican immigrant. They (police) were going to shoot me. I found a hiding place in a very, very tight corner of an old, old building, or barn, or shack. They saw me. I ran again.

In this dream the countries were set out something like this:

*this was
either spain or
a place like spain
where people spoke spanish*

Oh, I remember how this fit into the rest of my dream! This was actually the first part of the dream. I was trying to go <u>back</u> to Mexico so I can feel safe. But I didn't quite reach it. I reached the chain-link fence gate and had to turn around.

FEBRUARY 27, 1990

God, you are my Creator, Father, Love, Friend, Teacher. I love you. Amen!

MARCH 19, 1990

I am sad.

APRIL 23, 1990

Life is full of many disappointments. But I didn't think there would be so many in so many aspects: love, sex, friends, God, self, truth, jobs, causes. Billy Joel has a line in a song, "I once believed in causes too. I had my pointless point of view and life went on no matter who was wrong or right." I guess I feel similar. He also says that "just surviving was a noble fight."

With so many disappointments, that's the only thing left to do. I guess Shakespeare wasn't too far off when he said "To be or Not to be…" It seems that life is merely Being and nothing more. Imagine that. I am only a <u>verb</u>. I am a Be-ing. I am an action, not a thing. Therefore I probably don't really exist except in the form of an action. I am. He is. We are.

Humans are only a state of a verb, a motion or perhaps a *transition*. I guess I have yet to find out. And I hope that won't be a disappointment.

My Room
vista [ane
SLO

MAY 17, 1990

(2:30 AM)

Well, I just got back from the Grad [dance club]. It wasn't as exciting this time. People seem raunchier. It was a meat market. I don't' like that place. I almost felt guilty having Angela, Kenneth, and especially Amanda at the place. At least this time I didn't lose too much control. The music always seems to haunt me. I love it and I hate it. It feels good to be moving to the beats of the music…being synchronized with it. But I don't like the fact that soon enough, the music controls me. Like I said I had more control this time. Maybe next time I'll have full control. So I probably won't go again. I don't think I really want to. Maybe it's my growing up but things are changing around me (I'm probably the one changing). I suppose in a way I feel more secure of myself. I was thinking (while dancing) I made so many mistakes in the mere 24 years of living… falling down, burning my hand on the stove, stealing things, bad purchases, and in particular…relationships—relationships with family, with friends, with girlfriends. All this makes me sort of withdrawn and detached. Perhaps this is where my security comes from. Right now I'm having a hard time trying to detach my feelings for Amanda. I mean I am tired of boyfriend-girlfriend relationships. Not that I don't want it; just that I want it right and don't want to rush it.

My immediate desire/need is really just a close friend, someone I could talk to about my everything: God, sin, sex, pain/pleasure, love, desires and needs, loneliness,... someone I could give my time to. I want to care for someone. Right now a little puppy dog would be nice.

Anyway, about Amanda, I don't want to get her into something she won't be comfortable with. I most certainly would rather have her as a permanent friend than a temporary girlfriend. And that's the way I'll leave it for now. Forgive me Amanda if in any way I made you feel uncomfortable.

MAY 17, 1990

(3:03 AM)

Correction for (January-7-90) "Passion is a multitude of failures overcome by the continual desire for success."

MAY 27, 1990

Things seem out of context. I feel a little disoriented. It's 6:35 PM, raining outside. I feel numb. Is anything real?

I finally got back from Trey's graduation yesterday. Unfortunately, I couldn't get him a real present. The ceremony was hot and I couldn't see a thing. After that, we went to Barkly's in La Cañada for lunch / Trey's friend Sherry's house for the graduation party / then back to La Cañada for dinner at the Country Club. All this time, it seemed Trey and I had less to talk about. I wanted to talk about things more in-depth...about people, and personal problems and joys. But all I could get out of him was a word or two about an antique and what era it came from. It's getting harder to talk to him. I feel like sometimes I'm talking to a clay bowl...shaped by his father's ideas and colored by his mother's glaze. I want to talk to Trey. But I don't think such a person exists. All that exists inside the glaze and shape is dust that holds it together (the clay). Am I just bad at maintaining old friends—Or just not good at making new ones?

Changes are strange things. Sometimes they can be so scary. And sometimes they are so exciting. I guess this is so because changes are a transitional/in between period…like a chemical reaction…when a raw egg is cracked onto a hot frying pan, the egg solidifies…into something new…but between the raw state and the cooked state, there is the sizzling state. This is the change state where action takes place. If it were a person being fried there would be pain. Or more realistically sizzling in forms of anticipation, depression, confusion, and possibly even anger. I feel like this right now. With my job situation, I'm in anticipation. With Trey, I'm in confusion and a little sadness. (Luckily, God does not change. Otherwise I would be thoroughly confused).

I oftentimes think of that poem I wrote once… "People are like telephone poles on the way to paradise." They come and go, come and go. Same with situations, be it good or bad, they come and go, come and go. But what stays are the changes themselves and not the things that it had become or the things it had once been.

I mean I've been living about 24 years. I have seen things come and go and the same with friends and people. I guess that's why families are important as well as close friends. But what has stayed are the scars and healings of the changes…i.e. joys, pains, exhilarations, etc. It almost seems that what appears permanent is temporary and what appears temporary is actually permanent. Huh?

JUNE 11, 1990

(10:42 PM)

I just got back from the study break with The Bible study group. It seems that people in Bible studies I meet are people who seem to come and go…telephone poles. It's too bad. I guess the activities that are done, are done with the wall (barrier) in our head, i.e. "it's a Bible study activity and not a real friendship activity." Perhaps it's my own thinking… it probably is. In any case, I'm thinking this way because I'm moving again. School is just about over for this year. I always seem to get stressed out when I move. For me, I'm saddened by the fact that I haven't found what I'm looking for; not in this town. Two, I'm in a way looking forward to moving—maybe 'cause I can find it in my next destination. I doubt I'll find anything in Laytonville and I won't be in Humboldt long enough to establish anything. But heck, life goes on… white lilies.

1991 Creative or Created?

JANUARY 7, 1991

Everyone I meet reminds me of somebody else. I don't know why you don't remind me of <u>you</u>.

[illustration-Mustang Drive, Cal Poly]

JANUARY 22, 1991

(WEEK AFTER THE BOMBING COMMENCEMENT OF IRAQ)

I think that people have many loves, but only one passion. But why should my passion be sorrow?

I suppose I should focus my passionate energy into something more productive, such as design. Sometimes I think I love design more than I love myself—Maybe because my designs are extensions of ideas, ideas that are perfect in its pure form. I am not an idea, only human; full of imperfections. And because of this is so, I have to give into my emotions and desires. This sounds silly but… I miss me. Where are you (am I)?

MAY 6, 1991

It's beautiful here in Montana de Oro.

I feel now more peaceful than I did a little while ago. I'm also very hungry—another sign of dependence on my body. It's unfortunate that I can't record the sound of the waves into this book. It's sort of reassuring though of my existence and ultimately my non-existence. The huge rocks on the side of the hill are pounded by water and eventually turn into sand. No matter how mighty, there is something mightier that will make you fall or crumble. I guess I fell today.

I don't think the cause was Hitomi's designs or Dina's kindness. I think I was (once again) disillusioned with my own *expectations* of myself and my *interpretations* of life, people, and perhaps desires. I guess I still want to believe that I can have it all—not necessarily material things, but *everything*. I suppose in a way I still believe that. Dreams: people don't think that they can go to school for so long and then collect garbage as an occupation—nor do they think that with only a Bachelor's degree they can become the ruler of the world. (not that I want to collect garbage nor rule the world, but "somebody's gotta do it." —whether it's collecting garbage or becoming a top notch designer.)

I must admit however that I still do feel a little lonely. Now I'm very hungry. I must go and cook Chicken Alfredo.

MAY 10, 1991

[Illustration-melting ice cream on pedestal]

The other day I was walking home and saw a scoop of ice cream that had apparently fallen out of a cone. It was Vanilla (looked like) and was melting down the black concrete road. It seemed very symbolic. I could see a child holding an empty ice cream cone looking down by his feet at the remnants of his once desired fancy—A trite example perhaps to illustrate a more symbolic meaning. Since I seem to be writing a lot about disappointments one should already guess… of course! The ice cream represents lost dreams or perhaps just plans not working out. It was especially symbolic because of the contrasts. For example, the ice cream was white (innocence, purity, perhaps naiveté); the concrete (asphalt actually) was black (the darkness of the world, etc.). Ice cream was cold. The ground was hot. The ice cream melted in the hot sun on the unforgiving ground.

The pedestal is obvious. Sometimes we put things, people, or dreams on a pedestal. We glorify things. We admire them. We want to be a part of them. But "the dream has gone but the baby's real."

Gifts are strange things. I have discovered recently (through an anthropology article on reciprocity)—something about myself and gift giving, or just giving in general. In reciprocity, a gift is given with an expectation of getting something in return—for example, giving some-body a birthday present and then expecting to get one on your own birthday. This doesn't mean "I *must* get something in return!" You just more or less expect it to happen to you when your birthday comes around.

But even birthday exchanges have a form of calculation. I found this to be true for myself—only much deeper in my motives. (…I feel very withdrawn right now…)

JULY 10, 1991

I'm trying to understand myself culturally. I am born of one culture and learned of another. I went mountain-bike shopping and found out what a hybrid was. A hybrid mountain bike has a mountain-bike frame, brake systems, etc. with thinner road tires. It functions okay in either off-road or on-road. But I don't think it functions well as either.

I think I'm fortunate enough to live in California where there are millions of other culturally mal-adjusted people. It's almost comfort-ing, you know?

I wonder if happiness is the greatest thing in life to seek or have. Melina sounds pretty happy in the other room. What keeps those people so happy?

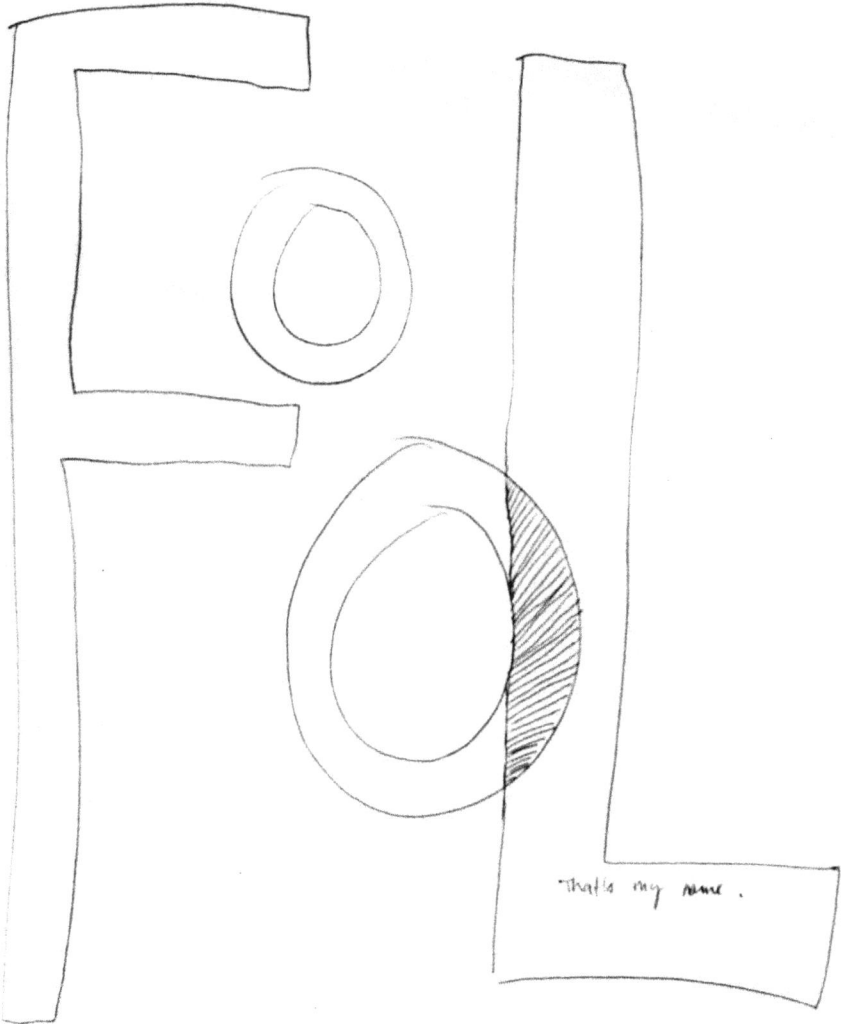

That's my name.

FOOLS ARE
NOT <u>COOL</u> BECAUSE
WE <u>DROOL</u> OVER THINGS THAT
ARE <u>RULED</u> BY OTHERS.
WHO'LL HELP
THE <u>FOOLS</u>?
Gee, I think I feel a little foolish.

Fuck you. ☺

oh shit.

please?

I love you.

good bye.

[illustration-innocence theory]

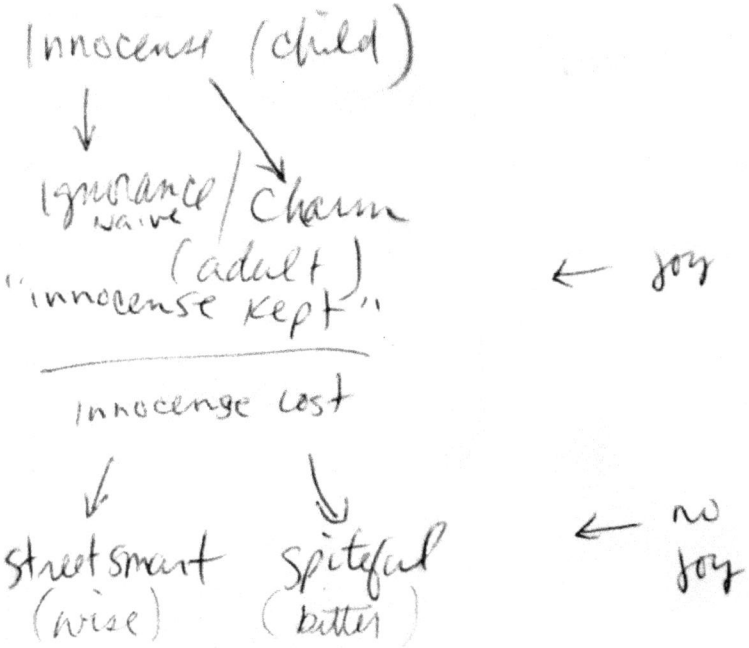

Innocence (child)
↓
ignorance / Charm
    naive
        (adult)
"innocence kept"
_____

Innocence lost
↓   ↓
street smart   spiteful
(wise)   (bitter)

← joy

← no
  joy

5/92

1992 Viva Las Vegas

AUGUST 25, 1992

(Tuesday)

Supermarket Glance

Sweetie!

Sweetness.

You liar!

Dis-Be.

But you lie too.

Victim of Self

Deception, oh

not me.

Pre judged.

Hole in your O-Zone

Layer.

Ten items,

Cash only.

"It is the green-eyed monster which doth mock the meat it feeds on." –W.S.

OCTOBER 23, 1992

(Friday, 10:55 PM)

I think I'm finally beginning to understand myself. It has something to do with "labels." All my life I've been told I was not much of a human being. In early childhood, I've been told this by many people and instances. For example, being chosen last for a sports team in junior high school—what a humiliating experience. Another one I can never seem to forget is practically being called a failure by my own father. There is nothing more that can belittle a person than having your own parent (own "creator") call you a failure. Mother was, I think a little over-protective… treating me extra-special. This leads me to think perhaps I did need the extra protection. This extra-special treatment didn't help any with my brothers and sisters treating me with indignity. Having spent the earlier part of my childhood as a skinny boy that got kicked around, I spent the next part of my life telling myself that I really was a loser.

When I was finally separated from my parents and family for the first time at 19, I began to explore who I was. Seven years later, I think I have an idea.

There are two major parts to myself. One is the self who still believes that he is the same insecure self and proclaims his *security* by reinforcing his insecurities. That is, by behaving insecurely, my self identity (the insecure one) was reinforced. The second part of me is the part that fights to prove that he's not a failure. The rationale is that by achieving great things, one cannot be called a failure—for example, my desire to have an awesome portfolio or get into an Ivy-League school. All this time, my reasons for getting into Cal Poly, winning contests and the like were to prove that I *can* do it, that I'm not a failure. It wasn't necessary for the sake of getting a practical degree in a profession, nor for the academic education.

And the reason I keep trying for higher goals is because I belittle my current status, again reinforcing my "smallness" or "insecurities." This behavior, the belittling, allows me to identify myself as the insignificant, insecure person. Thus, giving a sense of security. It is necessary to constantly belittle myself in order to *identify* myself. Essentially, if I actually do stop reducing myself, then I will find out where I really stand. Then I see how low I am and start setting another higher goal.

The answer then would be to merge the two parts of me into one well integrated human system. Do not degrade and do not upgrade who I really am. I shouldn't keep my security blanket by degrading myself, nor should I keep my security by overachieving.

[illustration-Electric Kazoo]
[illustration-transparent electronic ruler]

11-8-92

Electric Kazoo

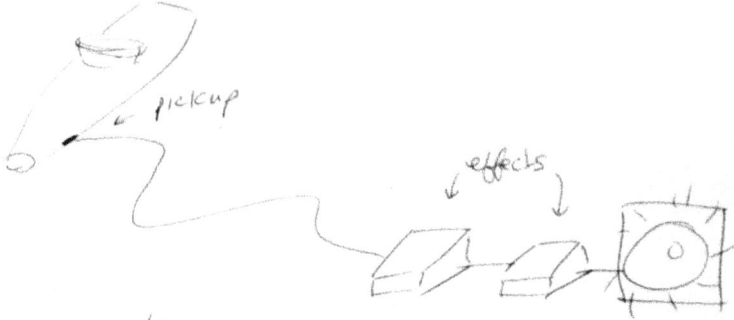

transparent
Electronic Ruler

LCD

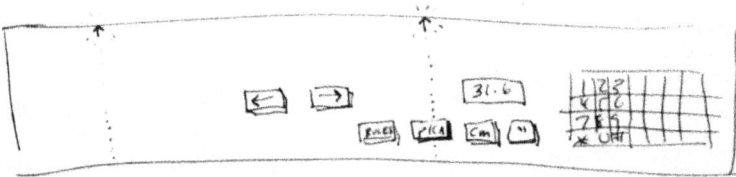

NOVEMBER 22, 1992

On top of the world—at least on top of Calico at Red Rock. Seems to be the highest peak around here. I see the entire city of Las Vegas. It doesn't look too big from up here. I could even see Lake Mead.

[illustration-Red Rock Canyon, Las Vegas]

DECEMBER 2, 1992

Who am I really?

I am faced with some decisions. I am wondering what the implications mean when I think about marriage. I have this idea that the person I marry will determine who I am…my worth. I think this is why I may be afraid of marriage. I am not afraid of money. I won that battle before. I know I can always manage my money. But there is something so disturbing about marriage. I think about all the personal sacrifices, the kind of lifestyle that I enjoy. Will that be gone? I feel as though I would be losing myself…the only thing that I truly own…the thing that took me so long to obtain. I like myself. I like who I've become, despite the flaws or insecurities. It took me a long time to accept that.

Now, with the idea of marriage comes the idea of losing one's identity to conform to a new identity. That is, will the new joint identity be better or worse than my current one?

It seems the only way for the new identity to be better is if both people would obtain their own identity while still married. That way, giving is really giving generously and receiving is really receiving graciously.

I guess it would be important for me to find a partner who knows and accepts herself…and is also aware of this fact. Perhaps that's what's most important in finding a partner.

I've read or heard somewhere in The Bible that when you're married, your body is not just your own but also your spouse's. I believe that's true. Thus, the reason exists for my fear of losing myself. I've also heard you must lose yourself to truly gain it. Hmm?

On another note of an octave lower, I may have a date with this Korean girl. Katherine told me she's a little chubby. I couldn't tell if I was disturbed by the fact that she may be chubby, or by the fact that I saw how shallow I was thinking. It's kind of strange how these things make a difference although they're not supposed to. Even dad was commenting on the fact that she was a commoner and that I was from somewhat of a royalty. I guess others' opinions do matter? Hmm.

DECEMBER 21, 1992

(6:25 AM)

I can't believe how much I am learning and understanding about myself and my relationships with God and other people. A Miss Trina Johnson with some minor misunderstanding (actually turned out to be quite an understanding) has reflected some insight as to my own nature.

When I started "letting go" of a few things in my life (like the need to be wanted all the time) I started receiving God's grace. Yesterday after church I went up to Red Rock to be alone with God to free my heart from my Earthly troubles. I laid on top of the mountain, as one, closed my eyes. The entire world was spinning around me to the point where I was physically dizzy. After the winds started to chill, I awoke and thought about how strong I was. I felt like a mountain, with God's awe. At the same time, I realized I could have fallen to the bottom of the cliff to my death. Then I thought about the phrase, "God can move mountains." I understand. I felt him move one yesterday.

I also thought about the part in The Bible where it says, "Let nothing movie you." I am growing like never before in terms of my personal/spiritual strength. I have God and good friends to thank for that. Amen.

1993 A Glass Menagerie

JANUARY 9, 1993

Lord, are you there?

It's me again.

It really hurts, Father.

I don't know what to do with it.

The Devil haunts me again with his wicked ways.

He's tearing me apart.

I'm alive.

JANUARY 10, 1993

If I love someone (a woman) does that mean I should marry her?

Then what is the purpose of love? And what is the purpose of marriage?

JANUARY 11, 1993

(12:32 AM)

It's occurred to me that I still have one thing left in truly becoming who I am. I've always had a low self-esteem in some ways. Being skinny has partly to do with it. As I realize who I am in terms of God, I see that I still have a remaining fear that I must overcome.

Before, I wanted to workout to have a great body and to feel good about myself. While this I suppose is part of the motive still, I realize it's much, much more than that.

I want to start working out, not in the privacy of my own home, but at a gym with other people. The idea is to face my fear of being embarrassed, my fear of being who I truly am, my fear of fear. I have to fight it.

I see that there really is no way around this. I can keep hiding and say to myself, "I am content with who I am" but the insecurity will not go away until I deal with it, face to face.

I am oftentimes controlled too much by my emotions that stem from my insecurities. God has helped me greatly in dealing with the emotions, but I see that I have to do my part also.

I have had this "glass menagerie" of a place to hide for a long time. I have run out of places to run to. The only way out is *through* the fire. Fight or die.

JANUARY 24, 1993

Lord, I come to you with my weak body.

Lord, I come to you without friends.

Lord, I come to you with nothing.

Lord, I come to you with only despair.

Lord, I come to you for comfort.

Lord, I come to you with my head downcast.

Lord, I could barely lift my face to you.

Lord, I have absolutely nothing that I could offer you.

But Lord, you feel my pain.

Lord you feel my sorrow.

Lord, I love you.

Lord, I love you.

Lord, I love you.

Lord, you're there when I truly seek you.

Lord, you are the beacon of hope.

Lord, you are my father.

APRIL 4, 1993

(Sunday eve after church)

Pastor David talked about proverbs and principles today. ...

MAY 23, 1993

(Sunday morning before church)

I must always remember:

Who I am.

Where I am.

I am a child of God. I must always remember and keep that perspective, no matter where I am.

A POEM

[FOUND A SEPARATE PIECE OF PAPER TUCKED HERE]

This silent and enigmatic
Tempest dissipates into the evening shade.
The black crow fears the air.
Not unlike the dormancy before snow.
Doves abound into armored silhouettes.
Rooftops are scattered throughout the cove;
Foundations have fallen into the sea.
It took away the child from his sandbox
And the thief from robbery.
Days were like nights.
But night turns into day.

1994 What Do I Want?

MAY 18, 1994

It's been awhile since I wrote in here. Let's see. I guess I'm trying to figure out what I want out of life. I mean, really want out of life. But before that, what has happened since I last wrote in here? I bought a house! I quit my job at KL Publications. I attempted to start my own business. I've gone through a lot since I moved to Vegas. What have I learned?

I learned that "friends" desert you when it comes to a woman. I learned however that a real friend can say "I love you" without having to feel silly about it. I learned not to sign any legal documents without fully understanding the terms. I learned that money makes people do strange things. I learned that people don't call you when they owe you something. I learned how to sail. I learned not to be afraid of other people. I learned how to listen to myself. I learned that dreams are costly. I learned that some dreams aren't worth pursuing. I learned some dreams are worth everything. I learned to forgive other people. I learned to forgive myself. I learned to call my mother more often. I learned that I actually like my family. I learned how to cry. I learned that not everyone is trustworthy. I learned to live in the now. I learned that people have a lot of hang-ups. I learned how to accept some of them. I learned that a little love goes a long way! I learned to unlearn some of my bad habits.

I've written two songs: *Winter Solstice* and *Angel*. *Angel* is being performed and (soon to be recorded?) by the Christian band "Under Oath." I started working out. I bought roller blades.

What do I want?

It would be nice to share my life and adventures with someone special. I do mean special.

MAY 20, 1994

(MAY 21, 1994 1:57 AM)

OK, still trying to figure out what I want.

SEPTEMBER 28, 1994

If happiness is what I'm after then I should consider this:

Dictionary: <u>Happiness</u> results from the possession or attainment of what one considers good. <u>Bliss</u> is unalloyed happiness or supreme delight. <u>Contentment</u> is a peaceful kind of happiness in which one rests without desire even though every wish may not have been gratified.

If I am to be happy, then I should attain what I consider good. This wasn't as easy as I thought. What do I consider <u>good</u>? The dictionary defines it as: Serving the end desired. My definition: fulfills the purpose of its existence.

Then for example, if love was the desired end, how can I serve it? Then can it be said, if I desire *her* how should I serve her?

I need to define who or what is good.

"Blank" Period

Oct 1994 - Feb 1998

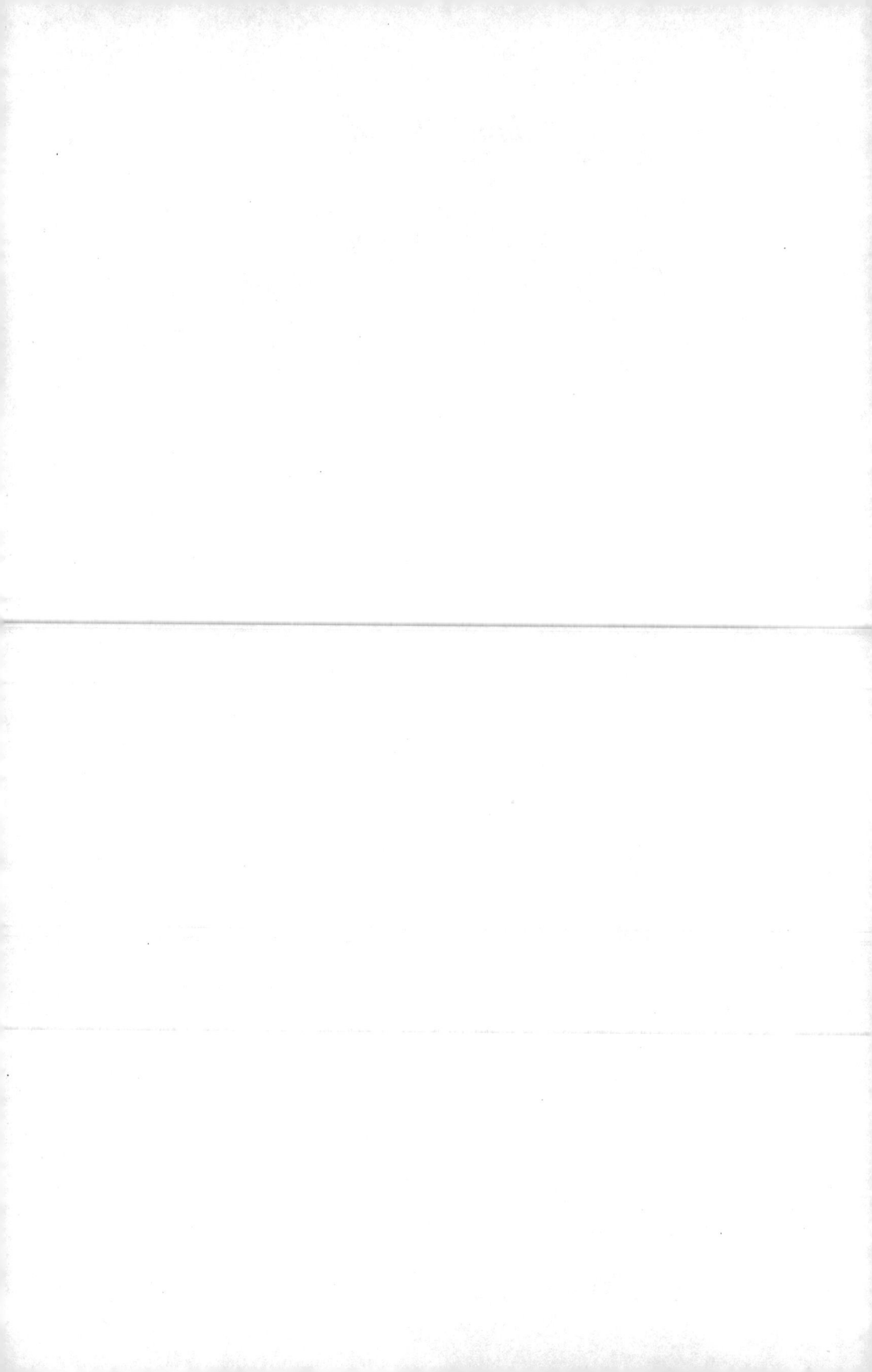

1998 Audrey

MARCH 15, 1998

Wow! It's been almost 4 years since I've written here. It's 6:04 AM. I'm waking up with a feeling of loss—that same kind of feeling one gets, that uneasy, I'm about to lose something (someone) valuable.

I've written a letter to Audrey in regards to how I feel about her. It's Sunday. I sent it yesterday. She should get it Monday or Tuesday, no later than Wednesday. I feel as though I'm preparing myself emotionally for rejection and possible humiliation. I think to myself that I did the right thing in writing the letter, in getting it off my chest. But I know this feeling all too well. I know not to make decisions on feelings alone. But it's the uneasiness, like the heart already knows.

I'm quite afraid, afraid she might say no, but also afraid that she might say yes. But either way, I'm having to deal a lot with myself. I don't know if this is going to make me a stronger person, or a weaker one.

I woke up feeling and (thinking really) a thought. The thought was, I'm getting older. No, that's not it. We all get older! But *that is all* that is happening to me. It's like a vegetable growing out of the ground. It was a horrific, sinking feeling. I saw a glimpse of what it's like to have a midlife crisis, wondering what I did with my life.

I'm going for a walk. It frees my body somewhat from the torment without ignoring or denying the situation.

(EVENING 9:00 PM)

I'm feeling much better than I did this morning. I know the things I will have to deal with is still there. In fact, in about 12 hours from now, I will be facing them directly. I'm not running away—which is a good sign. I'm learning to face my anxieties straight on. I think the thing that is helping most is my willingness to deal in reality and facts.

That has been a tremendous help. Though I'm not perfectly calm, I'm pretty close in the midst of potential disasters to come. Tonight, I had also called Lauren. She's doing fine. I asked her if she was married yet. She said "pretty close." I hope she will be happy. It was nice to talk to her on a friendly basis with no real hard feelings (not to say that the scars are gone).

Okay, I will be a real man and admit the truth here. Here is my dilemma: in the midst of liking Audrey, I realize already that there are going to be certain incompatibilities. For one thing, she's very smart for her age and yet I feel I will have nothing to talk about with her. I talk ideas. She talks events. Two, she parties hard like she's still in college... freshman year. I don't even get drunk anymore, hardly ever—just one or two drinks and I'm quite happy with that.

The dilemma is that if she says yes, I may have gotten myself into something that I may not have wanted to gotten myself into. Yes, I'm quite attracted to her. And it's hard to resist being with her. But there may be more pain, much larger and messier than the immediate rejection.

If she says no, then I will be somewhat humiliated, though relieved. It will be difficult to have my face shown around the office. I'm still praying for a "no."

Then on top of that, I said I'd make arrangements to find other work. Come to think of it, I've never had it so good. I make enough to pay all the bills while allowing me to pursue musical theatre and write books. The work is interesting enough and still relatively easy.

Another dilemma of the "yes" is that if I change my mind about dating her, I come off as a yo-yo or hypocrite. Then after all this is said and done, hopefully we will still be friends.

MARCH 16, 1998

(6:24 AM)

Ah, I forgot to write the real dilemma. If she does say yes, she might say yes, but with someone else still in her heart. I had overheard her say to Nina that she and so-and-so had feelings for each other for years. They had even talked about it. But she considered dating him a taboo because he and his girlfriend recently broke up.

I think that Audrey may also be put in a dilemma with the letter. Here is a guy that is finally available (me). And here is the guy that is almost available (Trent).

MARCH 17, 1998

(MARCH 18, 1998 12:37 AM)

I can't sleep. I think Audrey and Tanner went out for drinks tonight for St. Patrick's Day. I know generally speaking that we didn't have too much in common, but it still doesn't help the fact that she's out getting drunk with him, and that it's still hurting me. The kind of feeling you get when you're being cheated on. I know it's not fair of me to bud in. I caught them in a conversation today in the scanner room. They were talking about something and immediately stopped when I walked in. It's too small a shop! My heart still aches. I cannot stop thinking about it.

They were both prepared to leave together, but to make it less obvious, she left first and Tanner hung around…duh…doing nothing. Nobody hangs around doing nothing, especially after 6:00 PM at Hansen Design. As she left she said a knowing "bye" with a slight glance toward the direction of Tanner was at, but would have appeared that I couldn't be seen. It just feels awful that they would, that she would do that so immediately after the letter. IT'S NONE OF MY BUSINESS NOW! I wish my heart would listen.

MARCH 27, 1998

(MARCH 28, 1998 12:13 AM)

Just got back from Harvelle's in Santa Monica. I danced with this cowgirl from Studio City. She's 44 years old—not bad for her age really.

Here's a perspective on the Audrey situation. Well, a week or two have passed since Tanner and Audrey (probably) went out for a drink for St. Patrick's day. Tanner must have said something about how he felt, or made a move on her that she didn't want or accept. There's a tension between the two of them. Whenever I'm next to Audrey, Tanner comes butting in…to the point where Audrey doesn't like it.

Oh well. Who knows the secrets of a woman's heart? All I know is, is that I like her a lot. She's pretty cool to be around, and I keep fantasizing about kissing her…and other stuff.

MARCH 28, 1998

(6:13 AM)

I'm waking up again with a feeling of abandonment. At first, I was attributing this feeling to Audrey. But I think it's much wider in scope.

I began to realize this when I started getting feelings for Clara as a mother figure, and Clark (of all people!) as a father figure. It's a strange and awful feeling, this feeling of abandonment.

Where is everybody? Parents are up North. One brother in Virginia, another in San Francisco, one sister in another country, and the only one that I talked to on a regular basis is now married and difficult to reach. My childhood friend has moved to the East Coast. And the rest of my friends have either gotten married or paired off.

APRIL 3, 1998

(11:17 PM)

Okay, remember the "potential disasters to come" from a couple of pages or so ago? Well, I guess the last week or two was the silence, and now begins the storm. Tanner and Audrey went to lunch together couple of days ago. Nothing wrong with that except for the fact that their faces were full of "aren't you jealous" looks. That really hurt me. It got me very angry.

Letters are amazing and powerful things. It must be done with the utmost care and respect. The consequences can be quite severe.

I'm doing okay. The uncertainty can sometimes be a bit much.

I talked to Renée earlier this evening. I explained my situation and asked for help or advice, or at least act as a sounding board. I told her what I thought about the whole dating thing with work. She thought perhaps I was "growing up." And it occurred to me how amazing it is that anyone who is really grown up went through what I am going through now. I have come to have more respect for those who are there.

APRIL 19, 1998

(6:00 AM)

I couldn't sleep well last night. I found myself waking up frequently. I woke up finally just now thinking that there was something seriously wrong—something I'm avoiding or suppressing. I remember being quite nervous on Friday about something.

But the fact is, all surrounding evidence shows that I should be completely relaxed. I only work a few days out of the week. I rest the two days on weekends and I work on the book on the other two days. Yet, I still feel my heart nervous and anxious. I must write down a few things on my mind, even though they seem trivial.

I'm about to take a 2-week vacation to D.C. with Daron in a few weeks. I've just done my taxes. I owed about $800 in federal, about $400 refund in state. My current balance in my checking is quite low. I may need to transfer some funds from the savings if the UCLA check doesn't arrive soon.

I've also been out meeting more women, exchanging phone numbers, etc. Wait! I just remember part of the dream I had. I was with a couple of other people. One of them at the end turned out to be Tanner. Anyway, a bunch of us were being followed or chased, ended up going to old concentration camps and eventually Tanner's dad stopped the chase with the threat of a shotgun to the hunter/chaser. That was the end of the dream.

I still feel the anxiety in my heart. I think I may be nervous about this barbeque that he's having today. He invited everyone. Audrey might be there after her Santa Barbara trip. Tanner was very adamant about Warren being there, probably because Warren would be the "neutralizer" he needs to be able to invite Audrey. This sounds like I'm paranoid, but I think it might be the way I really feel. In any case, I need to be able to write down anything without the need for embarrassment.

If this is why I'm nervous, then I need to "neutralize" myself to the situation. I just had a big sigh. I must still have hopes of being with Audrey. Otherwise, why would it matter so much to me? I think I should completely give it up. It's for my own health and benefit. As Daron said, "Let Tanner win!"

Then to the best of my ability, I am completely giving up. Audrey and I will never date.

APRIL 20, 1998

(12:26 AM)

Okay, I came back from Tanner's place. Good food. Good times. The truth is, I do hope to be with Audrey. That's what my feelings indicate. What I want to know is how I can deal with this constant anxiety. What I want to know is, is it okay to have hopes to be with someone and yet not act upon it? I think I'm making it impossible for myself to deal with things if I make such statements like "Audrey and I will never date." I think that's sort of an extremist's approach and also a bit inhumane to myself. The thing is, I feel guilty if I say to myself I will never date her but in fact have feelings. So, is it okay to say 'I will not date her' but still have feelings? I would think so!

There's another thing that's bugging me somewhat. I've been working approximately 3 days a week, 2 days off and 2 days working (however slow) on the book. I don't see a future with this for long. The days off are giving me some anxiety. One reason may be the fact that I'm alone. I find myself surrounding myself with other people lately. Lately, I've started talking a lot more. I'm being more social, and I'm enjoying it.

But the other reason seems much larger in scope. It has to do with what I said some pages ago about just growing old. I can practically see the time whizzing by. I feel I need to ground myself with a solid job, if you can believe that! I feel myself slowing and settling down at a tremendous rate. I'm seeking warmth and comfort, and company. I'm tired of running around. I haven't done everything—but I feel I've done enough. Dare I say it? I'm praying for a wife. I'm praying for a home.

APRIL 21, 1998

(10:24 PM)

[Nothing written]

APRIL 25, 1998

(12:16 AM)

"Today is the tomorrow I dreamt and worried about yesterday."

I finally slowed down enough to be with myself. It's like in the movie *War Games*. The computer finally figures out that there is *no win* situation, no matter how it played the game.

For me now, it means that whatever grandiose dream I may have, they all lead to the same place I am now. It's not a bad place really. There isn't this road you follow to get to this one particular place. It's more like a spider web of roads all interlocked and eventually running into circles.

In other words, I have no more places to go. I can travel to other parts of the world; strive towards some end-all goal, but the fact is, there is no end-all goal, no end-all place, and probably no end-all person. It's a little give. It's a little take.

I bought two art books today. One is on the paintings of Sir Edward Burne-Jones. The other is the book of Erotic Art. Burne-Jones' paintings are some of the most beautiful I've ever seen. The colors are exquisite—the subject matter quite enchanting.

MAY 17, 1998

(6:48 AM)

Woke up. Slept okay. There are some changes at work. Nina had her last day on Friday. Warren was also laid off. There are already too many changes for me to handle. I can literally feel a physical pain and uneasiness in my heart area. It's as if I am a child looking for my mother to hold onto. But I realize I have nothing like that. Perhaps I am blind. I feel as though my faith is being tested. I look around and things have changed. Mom and Dad are no longer the place where I can go to get nurtured—they're needing the nurturing now. All jobs seem to be without purpose other than to make money, to sustain life.

I'm scared! What else is there—other than to sustain the life that really doesn't make any sense?!

I don't understand. Sometimes I say to myself, 'I wish I had some friends' when in fact I do have some very good friends whom I'm not utilizing.

Everything I want to be close to goes away. Or does it? Maybe everything I want to be close to isn't a physical thing, like a little child cries when he is parted from his mother. Is the mother gone? Well, yes temporarily. But she returns. The child learns to understand perhaps by repetition or by faith (through loving parenting) that the parents do in fact return. There is something so *powerful* about the physical! Not even words sometimes compare to the simple presence of another human being.

So if it is a matter of faith that I'm writing about here, then by combination of my learned repetitions from life and the love and presence of my parents (to the best of their abilities), yes, there will be something new to come. That is what I need to believe.

MAY 20, 1998

(10:36 PM WEDNESDAY)

Just came back from the opening of *Godzilla*. Interesting to see that it's always the same guys doing the different jobs for every movie. Godzilla looked a lot like *Alien*. I didn't enjoy the movie. It was too long and drawn out.

Well my life is taking a strange turn. I gave my notice as of yesterday May 19th. My last day at the office shall be on June 19th. Clark was somewhat emotional about it. I was too. I'm a bit nervous about some of the changes that are happening. I just interviewed at C.A.R. Design. The interview seems to have gone well. I'll know by Friday or Monday.

I complained that I wanted stability. And I must admit and wonder if quitting the job was a choice for the better or worse. I believe overall that I have made the right choice. I have developed a relationship with him that we've somehow come to understand one another. But I've come to understand that, although I don't know a lot about what I want, there are some things that I really do want. If I am going to work for a company, the company should allow me to have some comfort and freedom such as health benefits. I also want a stable and loving relationship.

I must wonder though if I'm being unrealistic about the woman that I want. I really don't think I'm asking for too much. Here is what I want. I want someone happy. She enjoys life most of the time. I want a good communicator, somebody stable and secure.

As I started writing some of these things, I'm beginning to wonder perhaps I am asking for too much. I say this because I want all those things that I said and have it come in a pretty package.

Somewhere in there must lay a balance between what I like and what I can get.

Also yesterday, I took Audrey out to lunch. Afterwards I propositioned her on being her boyfriend. She said she'll think about it. Life is interesting.

To think first of all that not that long ago, I thought perhaps she was too…without depth. It's interesting to see now after a few months, that she is not really that shallow. I like her. I really like her. The best thing she ever said was that she liked old people. It takes a certain gentle heart to feel that way. I hope she sticks around in my life.

MAY 23, 1998

(5:37 AM, SATURDAY)

Psalm 23

The Lord is my shepherd; I shall not be in want. He makes me lie down in green pastures; He leads me beside quiet waters. He restores my soul. He guides me in paths of righteousness for his name's sake. Even though I walk through the valley of the shadow of death, I will fear no evil, for you are with me; your rod and your staff, they comfort me. You prepare a table before me in the presence of my enemies. You anoint my head with oil; my cup overflows. Surely goodness and love will follow me all the days of my life, and I will dwell in the house of the Lord forever. Amen.

Just a thought. I wonder why I had a big lapse of not writing period between 1994 and 1998. I must have had *something* to write down. Let's see. What happened between that time period? Going backwards… 1996 was spent in Pasadena. That's when I dated Lauren. In 1997 I lived on Cloverdale in the Miracle Mile. That's when I bought the BMW. The beginning of 1995 I moved to Laytonville. Mid '95 I dated Catherine. End of '95 was in New York. I think that was the time period (end of '95) where I started to think really hard about my life. Not everything was okay. I realized I didn't have all the time in the world. And I didn't know very much. The last time I wrote was in 1994 (September 28th). It's interesting to note that I was really involved (as I am now) with two central issues. (1) trying to understand myself (2) seeking love.

I could sense in my "pre-blank" period that there was this emptiness. I sought external sources to determine who I am as well as for the validation of love. I sense that I ran away from this emptiness. I went to a lot of places to avoid the void. I'm sure I must still be guilty of that to some degree.

I just read the entry on October 23, 1992 and I cried! Hard! That was shortly after moving to Vegas. I think moving away from family and being alone has given me that first glimpse at true self-honesty. I saw that I was scared and empty.

Also as a general note, with women, it appears that I have often put them in the "nurturer's" position, not unlike mother to a child. Why is that, I wonder?

I sometimes think about this. I think about my relationship with my mother. There seems to be a lot of blank areas. But a few images do some to mind. When I was really little I remember holding her hand while she put it in her pocket with hers to keep it warm. I remember also being put on a Ferris wheel because I pouted and whined. Then I got on there and was scared to death and screamed to get off immediately.

How do I feel about her overall now? I'll put it this way. After the last date that she had set up, the one where I refused to go but reluctantly did, she said, "okay, thanks for making the effort. I'll let you handle that now." She finally relinquished control over my love life.

MAY 25, 1998

(MONDAY 11:24 PM, MEMORIAL DAY)

I just got back from Las Vegas.

Awful drive back. It took me 7 ½ hours to get here to Santa Monica. I took a bunch of pictures for the book. I also spent a lot of time thinking about what Audrey would say to my proposition. It will be exactly one week tomorrow. Mentally in my head, psychologically, I think I'm giving her 'til the 19th of June. That's exactly one month from whence I asked. It will also be the last day at the office.

I really hope we continue our relationship (friendship or otherwise) after working here. We probably will—to what extent? That is yet to be known. I think one month is plenty of time to "think about it."

You know, 7 ½ hours in the car gives you plenty of time to think about things. One of the things I thought about was that in the midst of wondering if Audrey will say yes or no, I wondered too if I shouldn't be reevaluating my proposition. In other words, will she be right for me?

I thought about the things that I welcomed about her as well as my reservations about her. The things that I liked about her were her down-to-earth common sense approach to life, her attractiveness, her integrity, and most certainly her gentleness amidst the tattoos and piercings. I did also have a couple of reservations about her. One was that she may be too young. Perhaps she will want to explore more of her options. In which case I'd be out of luck if my heart got broken again. I can't immediately think of another one.

Anyway, I concluded that overall, she seems to have pretty good judgment and that this would be one of those things I shall have to trust her on.

…The waiting continues…

MAY 28, 1998

(THURSDAY 9:23 AM)

Went out for a jog. Then also went for a brief walk. I'm freelancing at home for C.A.R. Design. I think they really want to hire me. We'll see.

Oh yes, one of my other reservations about Audrey is that she is not always a good communicator. She withdraws a lot when she's scared. And I noticed that she's sort of passive-aggressive. Come closer. Move away.

I must think hard about what is going to be good for me. I've been abused way too many times. I don't blame anyone but myself for this because I had previously put myself in those positions. I do care a lot for her but I will not place myself in that position again.

flip
the
switch.

MAY 28, 1998

(MAY 29, 1998 1:51 AM)

Just came back from Warren's. After we came back from Hollywood Park, Warren, Cindy and I had a discussion.

Last week when I had propositioned Audrey about being my girl-friend I had also bought a pair of shoes that she liked. I was going to give them to her then but the timing seemed inappropriate. I told Cindy about it and she thought I should give them to her. Strange advice. Warren originally said, just forget it and return the shoes—the comment that I was expecting. But after listening to everything I said, Warren and Cindy sided that I should give her the shoes. Hmm.

I'm going to do it. It should be interesting.

MAY 29, 1998

(MAY 30, 1998 1:05 AM)

Just came back from a walk from the Pier after having spoken to Renée.

MAY 31, 1998

(QUALITY SUITES, WASHINGTON D.C. 5:50 PM EASTERN TIME, SUNDAY)

Bruce and his family just dropped me off here. I spent a day with them. He's got good kids. They seem to really enjoy their Lego toys I had bought them. I'll try to see them again in August when I come out here for Warren's wedding.

…DARON JUST WALKED IN… [to the hotel room]

Before I had left I had written a little note to Audrey that although she hadn't responded, we may be best suited to remain as friends. Overall, I felt a little hurt that she didn't respond as quickly as I'd have liked. I have asked around (Warren, Cindy, Renée) for their opinions on the situation. They unanimously agreed that it's not going to happen. I felt either she was waiting for someone else to come around (either someone new, or an ex-boyfriend she hadn't gotten over) or she was putting me under strict scrutiny. I won't be second choice, nor do I consider myself under trial. I am who I am and I believe I had shown myself honestly in the last 5 months that I've known her. Furthermore, I had felt insecure because in part of this scrutiny. All in all, I felt she wouldn't be able to give me emotional support when I would need it.

(Evening 11:58 PM, Same place)

I have to say though in her defense, in regards to that last statement is that she may feel the same way about me—that maybe I wouldn't be able to support her emotionally either. I must admit I do tend to rush things. I get overexcited and want it now. In part, I tend to choose those that are not good for me—or that I go too fast to even see if they would be good for me.

JUNE 2, 1998

(1:15 AM, TUESDAY MORNING, WASHINGTON D.C.)

Couldn't sleep. Although I was lying in bed, I guess I wasn't really trying to sleep either.

Audrey is <u>bad</u> news, really bad news. As I have laid in bed thinking about the last 5 ½ months, it's starting to make sense. She's very manipulative. She's working the rounds to get a guy. First it was Tom, then me (or Tanner), then back and forth. When one became unavailable, or imperfect, or 'something' like that, she would try the next.

I'm somewhere between being angry and feeling sorry for her. She's very suspicious and does not trust too easily, whereas I tend to trust too easily at times to women. And sometimes not enough to men. I'm sure it has a lot to do with the way I grew up. She lost my trust.

There's a lot to be said for age and experience. Her divorced father I'm sure has a lot to do with it. She wants the one that is unavailable. She's still probably blaming herself for their divorce, to whatever degree. So, when men push her away, her identity is reinforced—the one she recognizes from childhood of the divorce period. I think she may think that by offering sex, she will win the affection of the man she wants. She'll probably deny this, but childhood traumas have deep and profound effects for a long times to come.

I will know she is healing when (or if) she has cut her hair to above the shoulders.

All this realization is giving me much strength and affirmation on what to do. It is setting me free 'though through initially some toil. The road has cleared and I'm on my way. As for Clark Hansen's company, the answer is still Good-Bye. I have more faith in God, but I'm very glad I tied the camel.

JUNE 2, 1998

(11:38 PM, TUESDAY EVENING, WASHINGTON D.C.)

As I have spent the day on the Potomac River, and onto Mount Vernon, it gave me time to relax and let things rest a bit. As I have read over the last journal entry, I was probably right on some points. However in all fairness, she has her struggles as well as her strengths. But enough about her. Now, onto some other things I have thought about today.

As I have done some personal inventory, I had come up with some things that need regrouping. This includes the following areas: Upon my return to L.A., I shall concentrate my efforts on:

Finance: to spend wisely and to save.

Health: Continue physical conditioning

Spend time with myself, trips, etc.

Finish the book.

My lease runs out at the end of the year. I will not necessarily move. However it will be the time to assess, once again, where I am with what I have just talked about.

It's probably a good idea, like on a Sunday night, to plan the rest of the week's schedule. My situation, as corny as it sounds, is similar to that of Luke Skywalker going to that lone forest to gain strength and understanding, albeit from a little puppet creature called Yoda.

On another note today, I talked with Daron about my sense of abandonment. I thought back on some things that mom had done. There were few instances. The earliest was when I didn't even know how to walk, she had to go to Incheon (market), she left me sitting on the ground and I cried and screamed my lungs out. I didn't know she was coming back. That reassurance wasn't there. As I think about it, I don't know that there was anyone there. There's a vague memory of my grandpa being there. But it's hard to tell from my memory whether that was the same day or not.

Another example was more deliberate and controlling, however. One of us (I think it was Katherine) did something bad. Actually, I think it was Katherine that led us three kids into doing something bad. Mom threatened to leave us by packing her bag and walking out the door. We all clung onto her dress pleading and begging that she stay.

There were other instances. Another one was that she half-jokingly threatened me to be put into an orphanage had I not behaved. Again, there are other instances. I guess the point I'm making here is that these past childhood experiences have translated into adult relation-ships. I have seen myself use the abandonment tactics to control other people. This includes, especially includes relationships with women. In order to keep them, sometimes I caused them to need me by threaten-ing to abandon them. I wanted them to be close by pushing the away (only, by threat). Then there were times I pushed them away for real because I thought that if I got close, I would be the one to get aban-doned or rejected. No wonder I don't have a girlfriend. This must stop.

JUNE 3, 1998

(WEDNESDAY 10:51 PM)

Boy am I tired! Woke up from a tiny nap after a huge dinner at Ruth Chris' Steak House—Excellent Rib eye. Did the not-so-exciting White House tour and the more-exciting-than-I-thought Capital tour.

Something interesting was discovered today about myself. It has to do with my motives. For a specific example, I'll use the whole Trina incident. I remember with her I tried everything to get her to be with me. Even those acts that seemed good were really a way, a hope, to be with her. It sickened me that I had done this. More so, I had denied it for so long. This was discovered when Daron had questioned my motive about Audrey. When I had already written a letter stating good-bye to any romantic relationship, I had already begun to hope and scheme how we may ultimately get together. This has opened my eyes.

I felt some self-betrayal while experiencing this new truth of shame. I saw how this had affected my life across the board. For example, I had never really had an interest in politics. While it is probably normal to not have an interest in some things, when I applied the motive factor, I realized, at least in part, that I was not going to directly benefit from learning it. So why would I bother?

This is going to change effective now.

JUNE 4, 1998

(FRIDAY JUNE 5, 1998 12:32 AM, WASHINGTON D.C.)

It's our last night in D.C. Tomorrow, we'll be heading up toward New York, then to Connecticut. We went to the Smithsonian and saw the Air and Space Museum. It was quite interesting. It reminded me a lot of the times I used to build models and look-up and read about airplanes in the encyclopedia. I've been quite bored lately. The last year or so I began to wonder if that was all there was to life. It had felt as though that I had done all there is to do and all there is to see. But this trip to D.C. has actually opened my mind to some old things that I had liked, like airplanes as well as some new things that I had absolutely no interest in like U.S. government and politics.

I had also said on a couple of occasions on this trip to Daron that I no longer wanted to be a kid any more. It wasn't fun any more. Part of this means that I will no longer be as self-absorbed. Part of this means I will take care of my own needs and not rely on others, especially emotionally. Sounds simple, and probably is. Part of this means that I will look "out" more, like volunteer.

I think that's all I have to say for now.

JUNE 5, 1998

(8:05 AM, WASHINGTON D.C.)

Something I noticed about the kind of relationship I wanted. In reference to the latter part of the May 20, 1998 entry, I thought perhaps I was being unrealistic about the type of woman that I sought. But I don't think so. I think those things I wanted are quite reasonable. I made that statement "Somewhere in there must lie a balance between what I like, and what I can get." While that statement is fair, I think a different approach to my thinking might be better. For example, I think it may be better to say, "Somewhere in there must lie a person who is suitable, or appropriate for me."

That is probably a much more healthier perspective than trying to "get as much as I could" —like eating for example. Sometimes we eat until we can eat no longer. I think that's not healthy nor is it enjoyable after the "getting"…or eating… or the process is done.

A better meal is the one that satisfies your hunger; is tasty; enjoyable as a whole that includes a mix of food (veggies, meats, etc.), and leaves room for desert.

It's interesting.

A couple of other things to note: One is that if I'm pulled away from my immediate home surroundings long enough to the point where I have no control over some of these home issues, I got a much healthier perspective on things, a much more realistic perspective. Two, having spent (so far) 5 days with someone (Daron) has helped me get grounded as well. It's amazing how much that helps, having another person's presence. I may consider a roommate situation.

JUNE 6, 1998

(5:00 PM, OLD SAYBROOK, CONNECTICUT)

Visiting Trey at the Goodspeed Opera House. It's very pretty around here with the trees, the Atlantic, and the local streams and rivers. I just came out of the shower after having my hair cut in Madison at "Tony's Barber Shop." I woke up missing Audrey very much. It made me sad this morning. But I can't make choices for her.

The situation wasn't wholesome somehow. I'm not looking for perfection, but I do want to be fair. I was being fair to me—giving myself some room, not because I wanted it necessarily, but because I needed it.

For this Christmas, I want to design and print a family crest for everyone. I've been thinking also about getting a second tattoo, perhaps of a horse. Having looked at heroic statues in D.C., I was told that if a horse had all four legs on the ground, it meant the hero survived. If any of the four legs were off the ground, it meant the hero died in battle. I just want a horse only, not sure whether all fours on ground, or the two front legs up in the air.

JUNE 9, 1998

(9:19 AM, BACK HOME IN SANTA MONICA)

One thing I noticed when I couldn't "go" anywhere, I was forced to work out some internal issues which I would have avoided normally—which brings me to my next topic, Hansen Design.

In having learned about my "motive factor" I must consider my reasons for leaving Hansen. Number one, the Audrey factor: Although I had weighed this out carefully before, she was not the reason I was leaving Hansen—although it gave me tremendous hopes to be dating her. Two, my reasoning, as stated to Clark was that I was looking for stability in a company, that which his didn't have. Three, I was angry at Clark for being fickle about the initial full time job offer. He constantly backed down. Four, having thought about why I left originally: because he was being emotionally irrational to me totally unnecessarily. I would not put up with that. Five, is my leaving for advancement in my "career" or is it for a better surrounding?

JUNE 11, 1998

THURSDAY (FRIDAY JUNE 12, 1998, 12:04 AM)

Just came back from a brief walk. I talked to Audrey tonight to clarify a few things. I started with the letter. She stated that she had already stated she did not want to pursue a relationship with me. But I did confront her on giving me a lot of mixed signals. She admitted that she did do that.

I scared her away. She scared me too. I told her that sometimes I get overexcited when I like someone—which brings me to what I want to discuss.

It never occurred to me that there are some things that I can't change about myself. And I wondered tonight, upon my walk, if my emotional nature is something that I can (or should) change. This is a sore subject for me since this is one of the "big ones" that has scared [off] so many potential relationships. And if it is something I cannot change, then I should accept myself under those terms and perhaps forewarn those new to me about my state. Let's see if I can remember that quote, "God give me the courage to things that I can change; the humility to accept the things I cannot; and the wisdom to know the difference."

In general, I don't think I can or even should change my emotional nature. I think it's so fundamental to who I am. Why should I deny myself the range of emotions from laughter to tears just to have people accept me? That's silly.

At the same time, I shall learn to be moderate and balanced in dealing with the *spills* of the soul.

JUNE 14, 1998

(SUNDAY 3:56 PM)

I just took a break from working on the frog book. This morning, I woke up frightened—although I'm quite relaxed and feeling grounded now. I'm a little tired now to think of why I was frightened. It has something to do with the uncertainty of things to come. However, I did force myself to work on the book. That did wonders for making myself relaxed.

SAME DAY 10:56 PM

I just came back from a barbeque dinner with Warren, Cindy, Warren's friend, Warren's dad, etc. Hispanic folks are very family-oriented.

In D.C., I thought that when I got back here to L.A., I'd want to spend some time alone. Everyone advised that I not do this for reasons that I already spend too much time alone. But having talked to Christine (Noley), she concurred that it was a good idea. I think so too, to stay and have fun with friends but not be looking for a girlfriend. I think it is a good time to give myself some room to heal and make friends and observe. Although this method is not for everyone, I think it's a good idea for me. I need also to be away from Audrey for a while. I think that would be very healthy for me. The situation frightens me. I think I should stay away for along time. Unless there was some miraculous change, it would not be a good idea to see her at all.

I'm tired.

JUNE 15, 1998

(6:09 AM, MONDAY)

Strange dream. I was in Death Valley with some friends. Don't know with whom exactly. But I got a phone call there. I think mom was there too. Yes, she was. She was talking to him (dad) on the phone. Then she handed it to me. I couldn't really understand what he was saying. Then I heard he was dying. And the first thought that came to mind was that I'd have to take care of mom. And that this put a tremendous burden on me.

This whole situation alerted me to the fact that their expectations of me were a lot higher than say, Brian's. Brian's 27 now, getting his first "official job". Dad responded that he's still young and that that's good for him. When I was 27, I was constantly pressured to get married.

I moved out on my own at 19 with a part time job and attended school full time. NOT easy!

I've been waking up the last couple of days with fear and the wish to be as far away from Audrey as possible. She frightens me greatly with her behavior. I don't need any more controlling women in my life. I feel like I'm constantly being watched.

I also feel some resentment and anger toward her. I'm not sure why. Resentments usually come from not having a choice and anger usually comes from hurt or betrayal. I think I'm resentful because she withdrew her desire to be with me maybe from fears and/or maybe from her own confusion about what she wants. But in any case, I got a lot of mixed signals that scared me quite a bit. So, I stopped the game altogether with that last note. She may retaliate somehow. And I don't want to be there when that happens. I think that that is one of my fears right now. She does have a vengeance streak in her. I've seen it twice in her eyes. Once was against me when she went out to lunch with Tanner. The other was against Tanner when she and I went to the movies. She frightens me and she's playing too dangerously with fire. She's going to get hurt.

I fear her retaliation might be through Tanner—either through spite, or just believing that he's the "better man." In either case, if she dates Tanner, I know she would not be appropriate for me. I don't need that much anger in a relationship, nor would I want someone that picks a guy still living at home under the rule of mom and dad. Tanner seems to have good intentions overall but his work ethic sucks and is too much of a womanizer, such as shooting darts on Audrey's breasts and Annie's butt at work. I shall just do my work at Hansen for the last 3 days and leave quietly.

[illustration-in bed]

JUNE 16, 1998

(TUESDAY 7:27 AM)

I woke up not as frightened this morning. I am actually enjoying the days off before going into Hansen. Something's changed. I'm not sure what. Well, yesterday, I started the job search. I think I sent out about 10 resumes. I dropped off my portfolio at "Portfolio" and also at BD Fox in Santa Monica. I read somewhere in one of those self-help books that the Japanese have that "do what you're supposed to do" therapy—such as doing the dishes, doing work, etc. It somehow grounded and connected me.

I also woke up missing Audrey. It's the craziest thing. I called Hansen yesterday to congratulate Tanner on his new position at DEZINE agency. Audrey answered and recognized who I was. It was a nice feeling. I miss her. I can't help but be happy when I think that she wants to continue the friendship beyond Hansen. I want to hug her.

11:40 PM

I haven't been this relaxed in a long time. I called a bunch of people in Las Vegas to meet with them on the weekend of the 27th. That will be nice. I also called Roberta Roth of the Los Angeles Choir. I will join them next season. Like I said this morning, something *has* changed. I think a big part of it has to do with Hansen Design. I'm quite detached to it. Although I have 3 more days there, it all seems very irrelevant.

My mindset has changed somewhat. I'm looking to new possibilities that lie ahead, whatever that may be. I must have called about 25 different companies between yesterday and today. Most of them were pretty receptive to looking at my work.

It was almost as though Hansen was a place where I'd stayed to get healed; to train; to be stronger; to learn; to be patient; to be faithful—like I'm finally moving on from something, whatever it was. It feels good. I look forward to also finishing the book.

JUNE 17, 1998

(11:10 PM, WEDNESDAY)

I'm so full! I ate too much. Had a huge Rib Eye steak with rice and kimchee. Stuffed to the gills. Then after a little while, after a trip to deposit some money at the bank, I went and bought a small (relatively) watermelon and had some of that. Then I was still so thirsty from the steak that I had a tall glass of water. I won't be sleeping on my tummy tonight like I normally do.

Well guess what? Tomorrow is actually the last day at Hansen. I got a call from Michael Kraft at Intralink in regards to doing some freelance work. I start Friday and will work 'til Wednesday, I believe, then I have an interview on the following Friday. I will also set up something with Ryan at Freeland-Johnson in Burbank.

Oh, I'm going dancing with Audrey, Annie and Tanner tomorrow night at the Derby. Should be fun. Audrey's going up to see her dad after his back surgery on Friday.

JUNE 18, 1998

THURSDAY (2:45 AM, FRIDAY)

Tired, but couldn't sleep. Probably the combination of alcohol and coffee. It was a fun night.

JUNE 19, 1998

(8:23 AM, FRIDAY)

Okay, today is the first day of freelancing over at Intralink. Should be interesting. I feel pretty good considering I couldn't fall asleep too well.

I had fun last night. I enjoy being with Audrey. I guess I didn't just leave quietly. But it was nice cuz it did keep things light and left room to spend time in the future.

JUNE 20, 1998

(SATURDAY 3:24 PM)

Just taking a break from finishing the book. I'm very excited by the way some of the illustrations are turning out. Some of them will need more adjusting.

I'm also spending tomorrow on the book. Then I'll work 3 more days at Intralink. Then I will give myself that one full week to finish the book.

There's something about finishing the book, like it's something I have to do. Well, it's getting finished. I can't wait.

Also, this morning, I walked to the beach and had coffee and croissant there. Right next to me was this notebook. It was this man's diary, with lots of pages missing. I know he's 51 years old. It was interesting to read his struggles. It was quite moving. Of particular interest was his entry on taking risks despite the possibility of failure and humiliation.

Everyone is afraid of the dark. Each person has her own version of this darkness and uncertainty. One of my biggest fears was (is?) being alone and abandoned. Because of this I tended to keep people at a distance and at the same time I wanted them close. The distance kept me "safe" while the need for intimacy and closeness kept me in wanting.

Perhaps this is why I think it's very important for me to not seek a girlfriend and at the same time spend more time with friends.

JUNE 21, 1998

(SUNDAY 8:55 AM, FIRST DAY OF SUMMER)

"Paranoia is getting the your facts straight." –W.S. Burroughs

Strange way to approach the journal this morning. I wonder about Warren. He seems to keep people around to merely fulfill his needs, and then desert them when they're no longer needed—like Tanner for instance. Tanner gets him all kinds of software. The other night when Tanner was extremely tired, Warren insisted that Tanner install the software that night. I think it was about 12:30 or 1:00 AM. Other than that, I'm not sure why he keeps Tanner around. To Warren's credit, I think he says he likes Tanner like a little brother, to help him break out of his shell.

But I can't help have hints of skepticism in my heart… and who's to say that those with seemingly good intentions are that much better. I think Warren sees it as a straightforward economic situation. "I help Tanner break out of his shell; Tanner helps me with my computer." Then what, after that?

Maybe I should be learning something from that. Oh, wait. I remember why he said he befriended me. He says he liked my work ethic, and to his credit, he does work hard. Although I have suspicions of his intentions, I also enjoy that straight-forwardness.

Motives are all about survival. It amazes me to know how much we are animals. And the more intelligent and prideful we are the less of a chance we have for survival. I have this problem, in particular, the prideful part. It had always got in the way of things.

I miss Audrey. It's only been since Thursday. But for some reason, it seems like a long time. Somewhere between not wanting to get hurt and my crazy heart longing for her, I stand. I keep thinking how crazy I am because I'm so afraid at times, and yet my heart always longs for her. I miss her. At one instance, I think about being betrayed or something like that, and at another instance I'm with her.

I don't understand my heart. It wants to do what it wants to do. And there's (seemingly) nothing I can do to stop it—like I'm to know that my heart will get broken, but I'm supposed to let my heart love anyway.

I want to say that I love Audrey, but I fear, somehow, someway, I must be lying to myself. I'm afraid that she doesn't love me back and then again I also feel that she does love me too. I said it a million times in my mind and in more eloquent ways in my heart. It has slipped out of my mouth on occasions, but I'm still afraid.

JUNE 22, 1998

(MONDAY 7:02 PM)

My loneliness is so profound. It is beyond words. I know it's not like this all the time, but at times, it is the most amazingly difficult experience. I need to learn two things: One is trust. The other is acceptance.

I'm very tired and I wonder when this life of solitude will cease. Sometimes it's so quiet I can hear the running brook in the depths of my soul. It's difficult to understand whether it's a good experience or not. It's not a pain like a broken bone, but perhaps it is the pain of a broken soul.

I truly believe I am on the road to healing, but it is only through pain and a willing effort that I will get better. It will take a lot of love. I think especially in the area of giving. Also, more and more, I've been telling everyone that I'm an agnostic when in fact I am a believer at heart.

I love Audrey, but I begin to question my need for saying it. I must certainly ask myself how unselfish is it by saying it, or not saying it. How do you tell somebody you love her without frightening her away? And by the mere asking of the latter question, one must be suspicious.

Why don't I trust myself? That's a very odd thing to say. I think because my past experiences show that I had made mistakes. And if I can't fully trust myself, there must be areas about me that I'm self-deceiving.

10:59 PM

...and if that is the case, i.e. if it is true that my self-perception, or self-concept is a false one then that would mean everything I built around it , no matter how "honest" I was with myself, would be a lie.

Here's a question, if I don't trust myself, who is the person controlling me? It is as if there are two distinct personas. One is the core self. The other seems to be just one step outside the core (OTC), the one that tries to control the core. I wish the two would get along or merge somehow. Or it's almost as if the one just outside the core should be facing out into the world so as if to have an interface with the core. I sense somehow this OTC to be evil. It operates out of fear and/or laziness and/or other needs. The core just "is." The OTC seems to constantly punish the core for its (OTC's) own responsibilities. The OTC is really mean and controlling. It's as if (and only if) the core has voiced its pain that I'm allowed to cry.

How do I get that OTC to leave the core alone? And now, who is the decision-maker now, as I, the *writer* should tell the OTC to stop controlling the core?

And the more I analyze, the more voices there are. And this "voice of reason" really in fact seems to be a voice of madness.

How do I let go?

JUNE 23, 1998

(TUESDAY 6:45 AM)

Again, I woke up with a feeling of emptiness. I woke up thinking about Warren and Audrey and Tanner. And suddenly I sense this wall between myself and all of them—like I'm being watched and talked about as a specimen. There is this certain separation between myself and the world in which I'm surrounded by. For example, at Intralink, I get strange vibes from people (except for Michael Kraft) like I'm some foreigner. The couple of Asian ladies there seem to be more warm and receptive. And lately, I sense this feeling of separation everywhere.

I'm getting a sick-to-my-stomach feeling as I have uncovered something I hadn't before. It's almost as if I had put myself into the "white" situations so as to be in a position of abandonment. I feel like I'm just waking up to the hidden, unsaid, underlying truth about racism, or at least racial differences. I never really saw the walls of separations before. It's giving me the creeps as I write. My heart sinks to think that this is at times how I've been viewed, as the "them"—as if to be tolerating me.

In Los Angeles, there isn't this "oneness" among the races like some other places (Hawaii for example) or perhaps even San Francisco. I feel pushed out, perhaps chased out like in a feeling of being chased out of the Garden of Eden.

There is this undercurrent here in Los Angeles of tension between the races and of money and power. The city as I see it for the first time, is headed in a "crash and burn" direction. It's a volatile city. I started realizing this at Intralink where everyone is white, or the iconified Asian Woman (sex object really). It's an image thing. I'm really getting sick to my stomach. My heart is breaking!

Perhaps this separation in part is a result of my wanting to be like them. For whatever reason, I think I'm in denial of my "Koreanness." It felt, looking back, it started around the time we moved back to La Crescenta. That's when I started getting sad—at Rosemont Junior High School.

I hope I won't start getting angry with white people. Although some of it was externally provoked, I must have a lot to do with it.

I think this one woman put it best when she blurted out her anger at me while I was working at Mom and Dad's store, "why don't you go back to where you came from?!"

Why don't I?

Because where I came from seems to be in two places: one is Korea, the other is the U.S. But I think aside from geography, where I came from must be my family.

I don't honestly think that Warren, Tanner and Audrey are pushing me away as so much that there's an obvious difference that I'm not acknowledging—that denial I think is probably a contributing factor. It's as though the "trust and acceptance" should apply to me. I don't know if one can completely trust and accept oneself, but I believe I do need to have a greater range of this for myself.

JUNE 23, 1998

(TUESDAY EVENING 10:02 PM)

Just returned from my Interpersonal Communications class. I haven't decided if it was a waste of time or not. I have a feeling it may be too superficial for what I need. I set up my first meeting with a Psychiatrist through Kaiser.

I'm getting strange vibes from Audrey, Tanner and Annie, (and Warren too though not as much)—a strange intuition. It's a strange feeling. Although I won't judge completely on feelings alone, I must wonder. How would they see me? I think they might say something like, "he's a nice guy but he's too wishy-washy." I feel like they're bonding together while talking about me. I feel funny. A thought occurred to me today. They're betting on whether I was going to call or not. I'm beginning to not like them very much. I don't feel welcome anymore. It was a very unprofessional atmosphere.

To tell you the truth, it seemed like it got that way when Warren got there. Having a friendly atmosphere is one thing, but that place was just too unprofessional. It was too gossipy. That probably comes with a lot of companies, but it doesn't mean I have to accept that.

Renée and Adam seem to have good friends. How do they do it? I think it's Adam more than Renée.

JUNE 26, 1998

(6:37 AM, FRIDAY)

I woke up with a new tattoo, a feeling of anguish in my heart and a thought that I should be basing my feelings on reality.

I know my heart feels this way because I miss Audrey. My being torn is this: on one hand, I have compassion and love for her. Yet, in my mind I think that

[Stopped Writing]

JUNE 29, 1998

(MONDAY 7:38 AM)

Came back from Kelly's last night. She's moving to Ohio at the end of July—kind of sad. I'll miss Kelly. Also came back from visiting the old Bible study group in Las Vegas. It seemed that most people had moved on with their lives. It was nice to see a lot of them—kind of sad, kind of happy.

I'm not sure why I had been so stuck on Audrey. I really don't understand this thing called attraction. Last week, I had spent some time with Renée. What a fine woman she's turning out to be. I believe she cares for me very much. I think Audrey's just young and she's going through changes herself. And how does one gauge love? Perhaps it is only to the extent of one's understanding of life, self, and others. Then with a good heart in combination of this understanding one takes compassion on people.

I believe I am loved very much by people who understand me, like my family. Perhaps all those times when I thought or felt I wasn't being loved very much, in fact, I probably was and perhaps it was my lack of understanding, like a child that kept me from being loved. A child I was. And a child, I no longer wish to be. To think clearly and to take action, not easy! Not easy at all!

And I wish to express here, in my own understanding of myself, of the need to, for starters, accept and acknowledge the love that's already there from family and friends. And I also wish to express my deeply profound longing to hold and to be held by my wife—wherever she may be; whoever she may be.

The wolf got separated from the pack. And at night one can hear it howl just as the Sun goes down, injured and needing care. Months go by (years in human terms, about 10 years)…and the wolf hunts alone, 'though not effectively, scrounging around for what he can get. His pride is hurt as well by the fact that he must do this. But it is survival.

Stay alive first, then worry about being a wolf second. The wolf tries to hunt but it is no good. He swallows his pride to stay alive and heal.

JULY 3, 1998

(8:19 AM)

The thing with Audrey is going nowhere. This is a fact. I kept fooling myself and hoping despite the fears that something would come about. But the reality is, she says "no, I don't want a relationship with you." In actuality, she is struggling to stay afloat so as to not lose control, or repeat past experiences. She scares me. I don't quite trust her. She had something going on with Tanner, which may be over now. But strangely enough, I think she's got something going on with Warren's friend Banner. There were certain nonverbal cues to this. Warren knows *everything*. It's hard to say about him because in one respect, I feel he could let me know what's going on so that I could protect myself. But then again, I think if he did this, he'd probably jeopardize his other relationships with them.

I feel a need to stay away from them, all of them. There are a lot of secrets being held, perhaps to "protect" me from the "truth." But the truth seems a little distorted. But rather than assuming all this, I shall continually observe and learn from all this, the truth. But I shall remember not to start with a false or prejudged premise. Because I may be wrong, I shall give them all the benefit of the doubt.

I am now in observation mode. Let me learn and understand these people. What makes them tick? I shall be detached to a certain extent. But I must remember that my goal here is to learn about myself through them. This …(I'm stopping my writing because I feel that it's not healthy right now).

4ᵀᴴ OF JULY, 1998

(SATURDAY 8:50 AM)

Believe it or not, I just came back from walking to the beach/pier (about 6 miles). I had a terrible time sleeping last night. Didn't sleep at all really. I had a couple of suicidal thoughts, 'though not too serious. As I walked to the beach this morning, I realized that my life had no real meaning. This is *not* to say that my life isn't worth living. I think it may be quite the opposite. For one, my sick curiosity won't let that happen. Two, I think I really do value my life, as meaningless as it may appear right now.

I'm wondering how I can make all of the things work for me, instead of against me. I'm very tired physically from the lack of sleep and spiritually from the lack of God.

Going to sleep right now.

JULY 5, 1998

(SUNDAY 8:20 AM, AT THE BEACH IN SANTA MONICA)

There are actually a lot of runners and bikers here already. Came back last night from Ron and Nina's place in Northridge. It was nice— just a few people over a barbeque and talks.

I just noticed how littered the beach is. People don't pick up after themselves.

At the party yesterday, it was interesting to hear what Adam said about women. "Women don't know what they want. You just do it and they love it." It was interesting because the times that I did have a girlfriend were the times that I took charge. I didn't wait for them to tell me to kiss them, etc. I just did it, and they loved it.

[illustration-Santa Monica beach]

JULY 19, 1998

(SUNDAY 6:27 AM)

Yesterday, I told Warren that sometimes I wake up scared. Yesterday morning, I *did* wake up scared. And today, I also woke up scared. As I have looked back on the last six months I had often wrote that I thought I needed stability. And I believe that it was this lack of a constant "routine" of things that led to this instability. While I do believe that some of that will help, I woke up with (I must phrase it this way) a gift of discernment. It's not about having a steady routine. I know that that routine thing at times leads to stagnation and boredom. Because I know that oftentimes, like at KL Publications and Hansen Design, that those kinds of full time jobs kill my soul—those jobs that in essence do not contribute to who I am, or what I love, or what I like to do. They are for the most part, unfulfilling.

Anyway, what I was saying was that my fears, waking up, I believe has more to do with a lack of TLC, Tender Loving Care.

Living alone, constant moving around, and continual bad relationships have led to that place where I wake up frightened—not in and of itself, but it led to not having some TLC. I believe there are a lot of factors that contributed to this—too many to go into right now, but some areas include: my upbringing, my initial birth's psychological makeup, my psychological choices, my fears, my creative mind.

I believe the single most important factor in this road to recovery is my mind and its choices to *not* believe in fallacies or faulty premises. I know a lot of this stuff have been self fabricated for self-preservation. But courage is overcoming the fears. I feel I am blessed this morning for this attitude and gift of discernment about this situation.

JULY 21, 1998

(4:30 PM)

I had lunch with Daron today. I was on campus at UCLA and got some literature on the Theatre program there—in particular, the producer's program for Musical Theatre, which there isn't one. Anyway, our lunch conversation was about why (among other things) I stopped doing some of the things that I had initially started doing. For example, why did I stop making films? I want to attempt to answer this question. There were a few things going on in my life at the time. Upon my completion of my first film project, I was having a party and screening of it. That night, Lauren was supposed to help me set up food and stuff. Instead she called from Catalina Island with another guy. That really threw me off my tracks. I had lots of suicidal thoughts then. I had almost no money—felt like a failure, dropping out of NYU and all. I hated *ALL* the design jobs that were offered until Hansen entered the picture. I was *very, very, very* hesitant to take this job because I thought I might come off my tracks; because it was *close enough*. It offered work in entertainment with young (my age) people who were "with it." It used the skills I already knew and had. It was a sort of temptation and necessity that I took. But my desire for change was still there. While I recovered from Lauren, dropping out of NYU, having no money, and had nobody I could really open myself up to, I did make another film in which the actress did not show up (Valeo). I had to improvise. The project did not quite turn out the way I had planned. There were also some mixed feelings on that since we were friends.

So why did I stop? In large part, I was distracted by the women that have entered my life. Another part was the fear of not immediately being able to eat or pay rent. In fact there were a couple of moments that were too marginal.

I actually enjoyed the process of *making the film* as much as the "film" or story itself. It was as though the film was a mechanism to facilitate my need to control my environment—not unlike a baby trying to control his. It wasn't about filmmaking. It was about me trying to control myself, fighting myself.

I stopped because of distractions (I think). I needed to eat, heal, and regain. I think as strange as it may be, Hansen facilitated that to a good extent until I couldn't take Clark Hansen telling me how bad I was, or his manipulations. By this time, I had already forgotten about filmmaking. I needed to be on my feet financially.

Having put together that first film, I realized the size and scope of filmmaking. It was huge! This is not a venture for people who cannot collaborate—which basically means relinquishing control to other people in certain areas of the film. I think perhaps I didn't trust other people on their abilities to produce what I had envisioned. This is a very important point. I lacked that trust and I lacked communication skills. I believe I lacked leadership insofar as trusting the "body" of workers. The head did not trust the body. I think now coming to realize that this is probably the area that has contributed to the poor relational experiences I have had with women too.

I think this may roughly translate into the fact that I did not trust myself. If I can't trust myself, who will? What that means is, is that I did not know myself. How can one trust one that he doesn't know—even if that person is yourself?

And since I did not know myself, I had tried different things to know which of my personhood's maze was a dead end and which were actually the path to the other side—the inner side. Like I said, it was the need to control my environment. And by producing I must be thinking that this is going to facilitate that need—that need to trust others, the need or desire really to relinquish control, at the same time control the situation.

Fact is, I would be committing a form of suicide by sacrificing my visions. But I realize, the only way to realize these visions is through the help and collaboration with others.

AUGUST 1, 1998

(9:08 AM, SATURDAY)

Today I'm having the International Potluck dinner party. I don't know who's all coming. I did invite Audrey, but she said she was already throwing a party for her friend.

As I look back on the last 6-7 months, we both did a lot of things that weren't very "becoming." But as I have talked (very briefly at Hansen) with her, there was forgiveness on both sides. I much appreciated her understanding. It's sad sometimes to think about what "might have been" but I'm very grateful for what I have learned. I hope we stay in touch and continue our friendship.

AUGUST 3, 1998

(5:51 AM, MONDAY)

Empty. Abandoned. Alone. This is how I feel. This is what I've been feeling for a few weeks now, mainly in the mornings. I didn't realize to what length and depth I've been involved emotionally with Audrey. But considering how much I've written in the last few months it makes a little sense. I've also been giving off vibes to my friends, the kind of vibes you get when you're heartbroken and abandoned and need some TLC. I need to heal. I have so many wounds in my heart. It's amazing to me how much punishment we can take before we reach that point of breaking down. I need and want kind and gentle people in my life right now. That's the kind of people that I always liked—Giving, sharing, and generous. I'm pulling my life together little bits at a time. I had gone astray for so long. To think back, I don't even know when that started. I think it was before Cal Poly. I think it was around the time the family left LA to Northern California. That's when I "woke up" and realized both my consciousness and naiveté. I was very scared. That was about the time I also had that dream of getting married with wet seaweed as the bride's wedding attire. Somewhere I read that this meant abandonment. I remember this thought even still upon realizing that, that's what had actually happened. All my family left Los Angeles. I was instantly "independent."

That's when I started going astray. I don't think I even knew what had happened. It was an initial stun and shock. *I don't have a physical family!*

That's the difference between friends and family. With family, they're always there…when you come home. Psychologically I think I was homeless for the last 12 years.

AUGUST 18, 1998

(6:44 AM, TUESDAY)

I've been seeing a therapist. Last time she asked if I had ever been in love. And I honestly had to wonder. My immediate reaction was, "of course." But after I thought about it, the closest thing I had was with Lauren. What I mean by this is that we mutually shared this feeling for each other. But as I recall, her heart was not quite finished with her last boyfriend.

I know I've been infatuated too many times. How do I know if I've ever had it? Janis Joplin says "you know you've got it, if it makes you feel good." Bible says "love is patient, love is kind, it does not envy, it does not boast." There are others, "love is a many splendored thing." "Some say love is a river...a razor...a rose."

I say "love is that thing, that impossible thing that everybody keeps talking about—that thing that rips my heart out. It's that awful thing that makes people do crazy things. It's that thing that everybody still wants, but not everybody gets.

Annie Lennox says "Love is a stranger." From my past experiences, that is what I say too. The song goes "love is a stranger in an open car to tempt you in and drive you far away...love is a danger of a different kind to take you away and leave you far behind...and love, love, love is a dangerous drug. You have to receive it and you still can't get enough of that stuff...it's savage and it's cruel and it shines like destruction. Comes in like the flood and it seems like religion. It's noble and it's brutal. It distorts and deranges and it wrenches you up and you're left like a zombie..."

Love has been like that for me. I'm afraid of love. I hate love as I have described it.

How I would like to think of love now is, "Grace and Mercy, Freedom and Restoration. The person is more important than this thing I've been calling love. It is for growth and learning of the individuals involved to become more fully and to let the other become more fully...

...their own...

...my own...

...without ownership.

AUGUST 31, 1998

There were so many wrong things about dealing with Adrey and myself. Today, I went over there (Hansen) and had a talk with her. I told her all the things I should have told her while we were still "cooking." I told her that some of the reasons why I behaved the way I did was because I was afraid of being hurt. It's strange. When you're afraid of being hurt, people hurt you more, whether or not it was intentional. She said she gave me mixed feelings because she didn't want to hurt me. She probably didn't want to be hurt herself.

3:25 PM

"A wise man doesn't need to prove he's wise" –Tracy Singler

SEPTEMBER 2, 1998

(9:45 AM, WEDNESDAY)

"Nothing forced is ever beautiful…and if it isn't beautiful, it isn't love." This is what I thought about this morning on the beach with my breakfast.

What amazes me is the fact that we have so little control over who we are, or who we're becoming. Although I read a quote somewhere that said, "Who we become is our responsibility." I don't think that's completely true. I think we are who we always have been and always will be. It's as if there was this ultimate decision either by "God" or one's self, during the incubation period (perhaps even before) that was made. And everything we do in life, we make choices to become even more of that person. And if the environment isn't conducive to this sort of decision-making, we create scenarios, sometimes sabotages, or simple justifications to stay a certain way, or to "change" a certain way.

And all the early fumblings and changes we go through seem to be a means for the person to bloom fully as the person that was meant to be from the beginning. And in the face of death, how can we say that we have control over our destiny except to accept it—whatever that may be for each individual. It would seem most potent to realize that who we were, who we are, and who we're becoming are actually the one and the same. And it appears that the reason why we separate the three parts is perhaps our own need to put our confused selves into a context, or realm of reason and mental sanity. When in fact, we are indivisible. Isn't it just our attempt to be living in knowledge rather than in faith? Doesn't living in faith mean we utilized our knowledge to its fullest, then acknowledging our ignorance (i.e. of the limitation of knowledge). And wasn't the first sin disobedience? And if our ultimate decision about our lives was made in incubation, isn't our current life a living hell or a living heaven? That is, because we have already made the choice to obey or disobey before our birth (and thus "the death" of the incubation) we live out our heaven or hell now. I think about someone like Nietzsche who seems to have lived a torturous life. That living hell was also probably his heaven because that was his original choice. It allowed him to live out his defiance, which gave him much pleasure but probably not joy, much knowledge but no rest. And I must truly wonder if there really is anything "beyond good and evil." That word "disobedience" has a few connotations. But disobedience includes, especially includes, listening with the soul's ear of who we are. I have heard that we are a composite of the people we relate to. However, I wonder if it would be better said to say that the people we relate to trigger those signs of who we are. Then, that is when we choose to accept or deny (i.e. obey or disobey) those signs. So the little control over our lives, our identity, our destiny, is the choice between accepting yourself as you or "God" has originally decided or else be living a lie. Who we are, is really just who we are. The "choice" seems to be a matter of acceptance. The "choice" to be "anything you want to be" seems to be a fallacy. Ultimately when parents say something like that to their child (i.e. be anything you want to be) if the child as he grew older, decided to be anything he really wanted to be, I think the child would want to choose what he already is, what he already was, and what he is already going to be. That is if the child is honest. For this reason, we shouldn't envy the rich nor pity the poor. We choose our own destiny, but the destiny was already chosen. Now is just the time to live it out. Accept or deny.

SEPTEMBER 9, 1998

(SEPTEMBER 10, 1998 THURSDAY MORNING 12:29 AM)

Today (9/9) marks the day I resolved a couple of conflicting relationships. One, Audrey had already been resolved. However, today was the day I said goodbye to Warren. He's quite an impossible fellow. He twists words and realities to deny his own shortcomings. I had always tended to admit my own shortcomings first so that basically I couldn't get any lower. The fact is some people just don't care enough when you're vulnerable like that, especially if they themselves have low self esteem (Audrey) or inferiority complexes (Warren). I had been sad about having them leave my presence, but so happy that they are gone with their immature and selfish selves. It's interesting. When you're honest, people are really suspicious of you. When you're lying, they are either fooled because of their own ignorance, denial, or masks; or they laugh it off. But when you tell the truth, people get scared. They all run and hide.

I think we must face our inner demons at some time in our lives. 1998 was certainly a year marked by facing some great fears and denials. Everyone has that third leg that they're denying. This was the year I took mine out and showed it to everyone. I feared that they would laugh at it…and they did. I feared they would ostracize it…and they did. I thought they would take my third leg to prop-up a table…and they did. I feared I would be humiliated by these people…and I was.

My third leg: perhaps the fear of being alone; perhaps my need for love; perhaps my fear of not being accepted…my third leg, *that* was my shame.

But this metaphorical third leg has taught me some things. First and foremost, I found out who my friends are. Second, I found out that everyone else has a third leg. Most of them are in denial. Also, my third leg reminds them of their own third leg and makes them uncomfortable. People will do just about anything to deny their selfish motives. Shame is a very, very, very powerful thing. Once you know somebody's shame (i.e. third leg) you have the power to completely destroy him or completely support them. Sometimes goodness may actually be in the heart. But if it is plagued by fear, self-preservation comes first no matter how good-intended the heart can be. "The road to hell (after all) is paved with good intentions."

Warren gave me signs early on that he was not someone I should be pursuing a deeper friendship with. However, my thinking was, "If we realize that friends can change, we wouldn't constantly need to make new friends." Well, that's what I was thinking then. Thing is, he hasn't changed. And I don't know that he ever will. I think in order for someone to overcome themselves, they have to make one of the biggest sacrifices possible…their own self. This means a willingness to be, if necessary, humiliated, embarrassed, ostracized, criticized, give-up the battle, lose the war, etc.

Lots of people have gone through this—people I admire. But a great deal of people don't or won't because this personal civil war would result in too many casualties. Instead they live in oppression and anger, a type of personal communism. They don't want freedom of choice. As DEVO says, they want "freedom *from* choice."

In a communist country, people blame the government for a lackluster life. In a free country, people create their own personal government to blame for their miserable lives. Freedom is not a country. It's letting that third leg breathe a little.

SEPTEMBER 10, 1998

(7:03 AM THURSDAY)

What strange imagery. It's a rusted nail [hammered] onto a wooden plank. That's the dream I had.

When I woke up, I had ideas about wanting, no…I mean really wanting to find someone permanent to marry. I thought about all the girls that are around me. And I realize with *marriage* in consideration there are very, very few that I would even consider dating—not because they're horrible people, but because of compatibility issues. Take Tracy for example. She's beautiful, full of happy energy, and has a "no bull" approach to life. I love Tracy. But I would be scared to live (wouldn't want to live) with her high profile life style. I want, definitely someone "international" in flavor. In other words, I would want my children to know, not only about Korea and America, but also about a third or fourth culture—perhaps European or some other third continent. *She must have grace*—a gentle elegance that comes from having learned to respect other people and culture. She must respect herself. She must not be cynical. No bull, but also no cynicism.

I do not think I'm being unrealistic. Yes the field has gone narrower, but I can be specific in my approach as well.

It occurred to me that she should also have an interest in something, whether it's dancing or sewing, or whatever.

SEPTEMBER 13, 1998

(8:03 AM, SUNDAY MORNING)

Since that dream, I've been giving a lot of thought to the type of woman that I'm looking for. There's a certain "home" quality about the person that I want. If I were to give an example, I'd say Lisa, the one I met on the wine-tasting trip. What I mean by the "home" quality is that the person is *centered* and living inside oneself. At the time I met Lisa, it was me that was not "home." It's the lack of game playing, or having to prove oneself.

I remember, when asked by Gayle La Champagne what I was looking for. I replied that I wanted someone who has already had one love and lost it. That way, she would be coming into the relationship not too blinded and more willing to make it work—not aloof.

The personal inner civil war should have already taken place; the demon ousted, or never really had (if that's possible).

I think this is why many men like certain Asian women. They don't need to prove themselves—although that's changing too. The timing has to be right. The age range should be closer. Lorraine was too old for me (41…I'm 32). Attractiveness has to be in range too. Daron wrote in an email, "with whom would you *not* have compatibility issues at this particular time in your life?" Lisa was ready. I was not. I was still immature. Kelly, I could be compatible with. But she's married.

I thought about the possibility that maybe I was looking for perfection as a reason why I would have compatibility issues…too picky…or expecting myself to be perfect—very, very high standards.

This is quite possible. But this can now be taken two ways. One, I'm looking for the impossible to avoid a commitment to something or someone (for fear perhaps "downgrading" myself—or perception of self). Or two, I'd say I have compatibility issues with most women that I know from a perspective of also knowing my limitations and strengths.

I think a great deal of compatibility issues come from knowing or not knowing myself. If I really knew myself (which I am actually getting much better at) I wouldn't be so afraid of the differences, because the difference would not change [me]. And the differences can be negotiated. And negotiation takes much practice and communication. And I wouldn't be so afraid to negotiate if I knew what I was negotiating with. And they would be less intimidated if they knew who they're dealing with also.

You don't get what you deserve. You get what you negotiate.

I'm amazed to know how much of my problems stem from the fact of [not] knowing myself. And last night I wondered if it was possible to be in love with oneself. "To know me is to love me." I felt I was in love with me. Imagine that. It sounds strange and twisted, but that is how I actually felt. I thought about all the things that I went through—the good and the bad, and I really cared for me like an old friend.

I need to talk more about me. I need to open up even more, knowing that I'm not going to change or shrivel up, knowing no shame in being me. I think that's where the "too serious" part of me shows up— when I'm afraid of who I am. What a crock of shit!

And I wonder, really wonder, if my fascination with musical theatre is just a means to overcome this fear; to let it all hang out—another important rite of passage if you will. A public declaration who I am, not unlike the tattoos.

The meek may inherit the Earth, but the assertive will be free to roam it.

I thought perhaps I was looking for the impossible to avoid a commitment to someone. I believe that this is true. But the person I was afraid to commit to was myself. I didn't want to commit to my own personhood that was not yet complete or understood. I could not yet accept myself when myself has not yet fully bloomed. And how can I be willing to negotiate a relationship with a partial "dowry" if you will? But then again, the blossoming has already begun. It's time to let the world know—not by shouting or making flyers and posters, but being still in the Sun and air, in just being happy being me. This is not the end of the growth process, but perhaps just the beginning.

From "Seeds of Contemplation" by Thomas Merton:

"You seem to be the same person and you are the same person that you have always been: in fact you are more yourself than you have ever been before. You have only just begun to exist. You feel as if you were at last fully born. All that went before was a mistake, a fumbling preparation for birth. Now you have come into your element…you have felt the doors fly open into infinite freedom, into a wealth which is perfect because none of it is yours, and yet it all belongs to you."

SEPTEMBER 16, 1998

(10:10 PM, WEDNESDAY)

It's a picture of a guy lying faced down in the hot barren desert. As I have read recently over the last two years, my journal entries, I made a few references to having jumped from a cliff into the unknown.

I have previously mentioned that I was falling through the unknown. Then about 3-4 months ago, I envisioned coming to the opening of a desert. There were no roads, no signs, no anything. Then the walking began. I walked and walked and walked and walked…until recently, I realized I had collapsed finally. That is where I am now. I'm faced down, with enough energy to know I'm alive, but not enough to get up, just paralyzed and beat—so tired to stay alive and getting sleepy and comfortable.

Mine is a strange existence. I'm somehow very thankful for my life, however bizarre. There is a certain level of joy and acceptance that I feel—a gentle toss of a rock into a pond causing small ripples that radiate out. I guess one could call it happiness, but I can't be sure I can call it that.

I think I'm actually living in my skin now. I'm comfortable. I really don't have to go anywhere. I am certainly alone, but I do not feel the terrible loneliness that I used to—not to the extent I was the last decade or so. No one should live through that. Then again, I guess lots of people do.

There is a cruise coming up in a few weeks. It should be a lot of fun. I can't wait. I'm also hoping to go to Paris near January sometime.

I can't help but feel clean inside—as if there were a lot of things that were dumped and rinsed out. That's how it feels.

Yet, it is not an emptiness that I feel. It's a feeling of being home, a clean home.

SEPTEMBER 22, 1998

(3:58 AM, TUESDAY MORNING)

I've been aware of my awakenness for almost an hour now. I couldn't sleep. I took a couple of pills yesterday (St. John's Wort). It's supposed to be a mood enhancer but I couldn't tell any difference. I'll give it a few days. Maybe that's what's keeping me up.

I talked to Renée on Thursday night. She said that she was worried that I may commit suicide one day from all this. She said that Brian thought so too. I had of course been that way a couple of years ago. But I didn't think that I thought that now—until she mentioned it. In all honesty, it seems I am doing very well. I think I'm coping much better. At least now, I realize at what level of reality most people live in, and it seems like so much work. However, there is this profound *real* reality underneath it all that just seems hopeless. Nothing really seems to matter. And yet in my mind, even that hopelessness, something that I wish to understand, is really another meaningless and cruel thought.

Physically, in the last few weeks, my heart's been feeling funny—like a strange (don't really want to say 'attack') pain, though not really even pain. I feel as though I'm in some sort of post war syndrome. Not a sharp pain.

Sometimes I think about Renée's old boyfriend that died of a supposed heart attack. Some people thought it was suicide. There are times that I believe he died from a real heart attack, not from suicide, but from a lack of love—a deep and profound love that he sought.

I'm afraid. I've been very afraid of things. If I could use a visual metaphor, I see a small child, scrunched in a corner somewhere holding his arms to protect himself from his father—to protect himself from getting hit. He's sort of helpless. But he knows those blows are coming. Then when the blows are over, he's shaking and hiding behind an alley by a metallic trashcan—partly hidden in darkness, too afraid to cry out loud.

I don't understand. I cry now wondering what's making me cry. All I know is my life is just full of tears; so much pain; so much loneliness.

I keep hoping for a saving grace, as I have heard it said so many times. But in reality, I just don't see it. I said to Mick downstairs that Musical Theatre is like my saving grace. But I wonder if I say that because I fear that I don't have one. It's a hope for hope—because I don't seem to have any.

SEPTEMBER 23, 1998

(SEPTEMBER 24, 1998 12:04 AM, WEDNESDAY NIGHT/ THURS MORNING)

I slept much better last night than the night before. I had a pretty good day. I performed my solo "Bring Him Home" from Les Mis. I butchered it a bit, no a lot. Tracy was being sweet by being a geek and applauded and yelled for me.

I'm actually up late, not because I can't sleep, but because I've been working on a CD cover for Amy Shanta.

I read a bumper sticker a while back that said, "I feel much better now since I've given up hope." At the time, I laughed sadly at it. And now, I think I'm somewhere there myself. And the funny thing is, I do feel better. I don't know that it's so much a feeling of hopelessness, but rather a thought that says, really "what difference does it make?"

Time indeed is really short here in this life—much too short to be angry at anybody; much too short to be afraid of living; much too short not to try some things in life that interest you; much too short to invest so much time in "becoming" someone or something; much to short. I am very fortunate in knowing this at a relatively early age. I think I always knew this deep inside at a very early age. However, my response has changed. Whereas before, I'd wanted to spend that time trying to put a "mark" in the world, or find some significance, now really, I ask, "what is the significance?" It's so tragically ordinary. Now, I want to travel some, relax, read a few good books, and whatever. It's kind of a strange thing to say, but I don't even think about sex that often. Of course it interests me. It's just not on my mind all the time. Things, places, and people are becoming very dear to me—not in and of themselves, but in context to life and knowing how tragically short it is. In that light, I value each moment that I spend with friends and family and acquaintances. Nothing else really seems all that important now.

I'm sleepy.

SEPTEMBER 26, 1998

(8:52 AM, SATURDAY MORNING)

I went to the Los Angeles Choir party last night. I met a few new people.

I've been waking up frightened these last few mornings. It's not a pleasant feeling at all. Sometimes during the days, I have to fight that feeling too. I don't think it's necessarily a bad thing. I think it will get easier over time. I think this fear comes from the fact that I did break out of my shell and the initial reaction is cold and a little abrasive. But like a colt, at first you stumble a bit, wobble, then he stands firm.

I truly believe that this is why I've been frightened. And part of this transition includes leaving the old world where it was warm, comfortable, and protected.

I have put myself out in the open now—ready to be seen; to be heard; to be loved or hated.

SEPTEMBER 27, 1998

(7:13 AM, SUNDAY MORNING)

Interesting snippet of a dream: I was in my cousin's old house in Montrose. That house appears to me occasionally in my dreams. It must have been a fun and comfortable place for me.

Anyway, I was in that house and I saw Audrey get out of the car with her boyfriend. I couldn't really see what he looked like, but I did see her. Her face was teary-eyed as she walked by the window. She was probably having relational problems with him. At least, that is what I thought in my dream.

It gave me a feeling of, in part, revenge, and perhaps some sense that, some hope that, maybe I was the one...she let go.

Warren and Audrey were important people to me. And maybe that's why I was so distraught over the end of these relationships. I felt very used by both of them; for both of their egos; their self-concepts; their lies really, self-lies that I believed.

Along with the end of the relationships, the "fantasy" got destroyed too, perhaps that fantasy about the perfect friend and the perfect love. It's all really sick, the things that exist in "reality." Everyone scrambling for what little there is to go around, or at least, for what little everyone *thinks* there is to go around.

People don't have the courage to doubt.

[-]

By the way, I woke up again with that feeling of fear again. It actually translated into a real physical feeling—from wanting to cry to an overall nervousness that stems from my central spine up toward my back and shoulder area. I need to be physically touched. I need human physical contact.

SEPTEMBER 28, 1998

(MONDAY EVENING 10:07 PM)

A few interesting things to note today: One, Warren had called me and asked if I can work 2 days out of the week for a couple of weeks. I replied "no." I'm very busy these days. I said try Jenkers since he was looking for additional work and interviewing at DEZINE. Two, Tracy wasn't in class today. I'm a little concerned about her. She seems somehow terribly lonely. Although, I was kind of sad that she wasn't there in the first half of class, I felt really good when that was no longer a concern and I was paying attention to the Musical Theatre class.

Oh, Warren said, "We gotta talk." I said, "Yeah, we gotta talk." Now, I have to wonder, why he wanted to wait so long to call if he knew he wanted to "talk." He waited *for me to call* to see if I would put myself in that position of "forgiving." That would allow two things: One, it would allow him to be the "bigger" person and be able to "forgive" me for having been so stubborn about being "wrong." Two, it would allow him to hide his shame.

Why can't people just say, "I'm sorry."? He's going to come to the conclusion that we'll agree to disagree and that is that. But the fact is, he'll hold onto it and use it later some time down the line and tell me how wrong I am about things.

Last Wednesday, the day I performed, Tracy said, "I just love you." It was a nice feeling. I said, "I love you too." I missed her today—although it was good to have that break from the routine. I almost sense that she wants to be rescued from something, or perhaps someone. In some ways, I wish I could fall in love with her. She's so easy to love. She makes me very happy. She has good life energy. But again, there is that boyfriend situation again. Nope. No way, no how, will I fall in love with someone with a boyfriend, especially a live-in boyfriend. But that will be up to her, not me.

SEPTEMBER 30, 1998

(WEDNESDAY MORNING 9:57 AM)

I've been waking up frightened and lonely every morning for awhile. Once I get up however, I feel good. No, sometimes, I feel great.

I jogged this morning—haven't done so in about a week. I hope I won't feel like this for a lot longer.

Also of note, the family is now completely separated geographically. Mom and Dad are in Windsor; Bruce, in Virginia; Renée in Fresno; Brian in San Francisco; I'm in LA.; Katherine is in Korea. Of course our lives are all more independent as we become more of who we are.

I wrote an email to Daron about Warren calling me. He (Daron) said that I was being too hard on him and told me to recall a certain friend that I lost (Ann) because I had pushed her away—and that I regretted that. Ann never manipulated my words or me. She was just arrogant.

Warren isn't so much arrogant as he is a user. But I wonder, perhaps, if I was being too hard on him. Yes the friendship started on a strange footing but there were a lot of good things that came out of it too.

And the fact that he called, at least, signifies that he cares—perhaps a little clumsy, but nonetheless, an effort. Both Renée and Daron seem to have found some good in him.

OCTOBER 2, 1998

(FRIDAY EVENING 12:35 AM)

Well, I called him on Wednesday and left a message on his cell phone, to call me back with his new address. He never did. He did not call because he cared. He called to have the last hit. Loser.

On a much happier note, I saw "Pecker" by John Waters. It was a lot of fun. It makes one take life not so seriously.

OCTOBER 6, 1998

(8PM TUESDAY EVENING)

it's interesting. I feel I'm finally on my own two feet, emotionally, physically, financially. It's a good feeling. At times it can still be a little frightening—sort of like walking on a tight rope high above the ground. If I don't think too much about it, I'm fine. But if I look down or think "wow, I'm actually doing it," then it can get intimidating.

I think life is about as good as it gets. I don't have everything. I haven't tried everything either. But I'm pretty content. I have flaws, I know. But I really am more comfortable in my skin. I think I'm interesting.

Like a lot of things, standing and knowing you're by yourself, is also overrated. Or another way to say it is, it's kind of lonely. Not really a horrible, unbearable kind of loneliness, but it's just really quiet in the solitude.

I picture an Indian sitting by the edge of a cliff. It is dusk, and the sun is no longer visible. The sky is orange and burnt. He looks out into the distance. But he's not really looking anything in particular. He just knows things. He just *knows.*

OCTOBER 10, 1998

(6:20 PM, SATURDAY EVENING)

I'm in my cabin on the "Holiday" Carnival Cruise. Geeze, what a party boat. It's like living in Vegas again.

My cabin comes without a window. But it also comes without a roommate—which is great. I won "The Twist" dance contest. I was video-taped and it was played on the ship's TV sets. Everyone started calling me things like "Mister Twister" or "The Twist."

That's my 15 minutes of fame. I'm having a good time. I went horseback riding today. Oh, and yesterday I won $140.00 on the Quarter Video Poker. I'm a little tired now and I look forward to a peaceful Sunday.

There were a lot of nice people I met here. If I do another cruise however, I'd want to try something more luxurious; something more elegant.

OCTOBER 11, 1998

(10:07 PM, SUNDAY EVENING)

It's absolutely pitch black outside. The boat is moving of course. But it's just dark out there. I'm in the "wharf" of the boat, a general eating area for pizza and late night buffets, etc. Wow, I just spent $3,000.00 on a Dali wood engraving...yes, signed. I never bought anything like that. I mean, I spent much more than that on tangible goods such as that home in Las Vegas, the cars that I've had, etc.

It was a little bit scary. But something inside was just very confident about it. It's my first purchase of its kind. And initially it seems a little outrageous. The man (the auctioneer) said it was appraised at around

$8,000.00. There were 25 of those prints signed. It should be delivered in about 6-8 weeks. I believe I am very good at judging art…i.e. the quality.

Hopefully, I'll make some money off of this one. If not, it really is a beautiful piece. It's called "Fallen Angel" from his series of 100 he did for Dante's Divine Comedy.

It also occurred to me that these people who have all this money don't really know much about art. Their needs can easily be fulfilled by going to a local art show (a lot of which is very good) for a lot less money.

I wonder what it would be like to be buying and selling art as a living. There are a couple of things still on my mind that hasn't been completed this year. First is of course, that book. That book that's been begging to be completed. I have approximately 2 months left before the termination of the year. So, I'll get it done.

That brings me to my next question for myself. I realize the time to make that next move is now. Not next year; not 2 years from now. One of my more promising ideas is the publishing company. I don't have all the details yet, but once the decision is made, I will have a firm grasp of the ins and outs of starting and running an independent book publishing company.

There are other options I've been exploring, one of which is writing and/or producing musical theatre. I really do enjoy musical theatre. However, in the scope of things, I believe it is best suited as a hobby. I have many, many interests, which is wonderful. But time is more valuable than money. It is definitely limited. There are some things I need to simplify and streamline. Let's see, some of the interests are:

- Publishing/Children's books
- Musical Theatre
- 3-D animation
- Music
- Design & Advertising

My most viable option is design in terms of the "easy" scale. The next two, publishing and 3-D animation come close to being the next most viable option. The other two, music and musical theatre, something I really love is best suited for "personal interest."

Before I came on the trip, I thought it would be most beneficial to do 3-D animation as a living and music as a hobby. *However*, again, in the scope of things and mine getting a different perspective on things, I believe it is best to start the book publishing company. When I do, initially, I will have little time for much else. All these things I've said, even without consideration to family and friends, which ultimately is what matters.

Design & Advertising is keeping me alive and well. So that'll keep me afloat while I make these changes.

OCTOBER 12, 1998

(2:14 AM, MONDAY MORNING)

Just got back from the dance. I can't believe I won 2 dance contests. Vivian's the Twister partner and Brandy's the disco partner.

Anyway, I wanted to write in here because it occurred to me tonight that most women seem to bore me. This is quite a surprise since I've been always so head-over-heels about things. Underneath the initial skin, they really have little to say. Most do not seem to have vulnerability or a sense of curiosity. A lot of them don't even know how to cook. It's sort of a shame. I mean with women now having more power these days, they seem to have become the things they despised in men—a sort of a shield to (or a loss of) being a woman; insensitive beasts without real passion. Just like men, it's still the *true* independent thinkers; the entrepreneurs; the artist; the writer, etc. that seem to be interesting…and that are still attractive to me.

OCTOBER 20, 1998

(10:33 PM, TUESDAY EVENING)

Ella came by to rehearse "A little fall of rain." We're having a little difficulty with the staging. It's not a comfortable position to be singing. She's a nice girl.

My perspective and outlook has changed considerably over the past few months. It's much more positive and healthy. I've been giving (gradually) more and more thought on Brainchild Publishing.

OCTOBER 26, 1998

(11:24 AM, MONDAY)

On campus at SMC: I just thought of another story idea. It got inspired by these Asian cafeteria women. The're so "short" and rude. They're so stingy too—the way they have their businesses set up. Anyway, I'd create these fictitious characters, say, maybe three "stupid" little people with much greed. They set out to conquer the world, or at least make millions scheming up a seedy business plan. The thing is, they actually succeed. But what do they do with their money and success? They make large idols of themselves that eventually topple over and destroy their village and all their tacky little accessories. The end. Hee hee.

OCTOBER 31, 1998

(2:50 AM, MONDAY MORNING)

Something is keeping me awake. My body's tired. My eyes are sleepy, but my mind does not want to rest. I feel worried or stressed out about something. It's probably in part this musical theatre class. There is just no rest with this class. Working with some of these young people is stressing me out. So much of this rehearsal stuff could be accomplished in much-a-shorter time. See, to them, it's more than a musical theatre class. It's a chance to interact with one another, to socialize, to play politics, to figure out all this "where I fit in" shit. Rodney needs to be in the center of attention. I don't like him. He won't teach the dance steps because (1) he won't look so "impressive" when everyone else can do what he does, and (2)—(lost my train of thought).

I see a few people's feelings in their eyes. Take Sarah for example and Jennifer for example. Jennifer already *does* musical theatre and she's not really into all that "theatre people" shit. "Aren't we so fucking weird because we're theatre people." When in fact, they couldn't be more mediocre and mundane.

It's not fair of me to bad-mouth some of them because, naturally, it's their age. A lot of them work very hard and are dedicated. But then again, some will stay that way.

NOVEMBER 1, 1998

(MONDAY 11:40 AM ON CAMPUS AT SMC)

I got here for the 11:00 AM practice with Ella. Apparently, she had called and left a message on the answering machine about 20 minutes before I saw her. she's moving from Santa Monica to Burbank. I don't think she's very interested in doing the duet. She has avoided it (the rehearsals) on a number of occasions. And this last one, she could have called my cell phone but she didn't, and she did have time for the other rehearsals.

I suppose, yes, I could be taking this all too personally but, I think she's just got too much going on. And given her circumstances, she's prioritizing according to what's important. I don't know if it's because of my experiences with Audrey and Warren, but I am now very short with people who don't respect me or my time. I just don't put up with it.

A story thought—as I have looked around where I'm sitting, I'm beginning to think that there are a lot of lonely men these days. Perhaps it's just an extension of myself looking in, looking out, but it just seems that way. Men are at a loss. Women want them to be perfect, according to their whim. And then those that are "perfect" are too perfect and need to change. There's no pleasing a woman except perhaps to please yourself. Women are not as smart as they make themselves out to be. All their smarts are still compared to men. And as long as they do this, they will never be smarter than men.

In The Bible, it is said to "live in the world, but not be of the world." It's really a lonely proposition but that's the way life feels for me. I live here. I interact with people, but I am detached and have this other "perspective" that most people don't see or are avoiding.

I need to (want to) travel a little more. I feel I am not seeing a slightly larger picture. I need (want) to be in the international circle. I guess that's my void I'd like to fill soon.

1999 Vanguard Advertising

JANUARY 12, 1999

(9:43 PM, TUESDAY EVENING)

I've been working at Vanguard Advertising for a few months now. Yesterday was the first day I started working there 5 days per week.

Rod is an interesting fellow. He's got no spine. I sense he's spying on me, perhaps for the owner or perhaps for himself. He's a tattle tale; a little girl, perhaps threatened by competition—or just my presence.

What I've learned over the past few years is that (in terms of work) a great portion of my discontent comes from working for someone else; the lack of freedom that comes from it. It constricts my time, essentially, my life, eat, work, sleep; eat, work, sleep, etc. No wonder people are always "living for the weekend." If people had all the time in the world, they wouldn't be so eager to live for just the weekend.

APRIL 12, 1999

(10:56 PM, MONDAY EVENING)

I just read over some of the past pages in this journal. It's interesting to see some of the progression. Take for example, my trip to Europe. Some pages back I said I wish to travel more and become more "international." It should be a nice trip. I'll leave on the 28th of this month and return on May 17th. I'm hoping my birthday will be in Paris. If not, it will most likely be in Madrid.

Work is "interesting." Now that I'm there more or less, permanently, it seems they're back to their old ways. What I mean by this is that I'm becoming another employee. Worse yet, the creative projects are dwindling. I'm doing more and more production work and less and less creative art and design work. That'll have to change soon—most likely, after my trip. I don't understand their (Vanguard's) structure.

It's a structure based on Stefan, Mark and Aaron. They're the "heads" of the company. But quite frankly it just feels like a lot of in-breeding of staff. People aren't hired too much for their qualifications, but rather by being related. And those that are qualified, like Marcie, are cornered into a subservient position doing production work. Zarah, the giant mouse, Jack the scaredy cat, and Rod the weasel work around me. None of them have talent. Rod is a good computer guy. And why is Louise running Home Video—the former bookkeeper? It's getting a little frustrating…No wonder the company is not getting creative work.

APRIL 17, 1999

(7:53 AM, SATURDAY)

I never really sleep in too much when I have the opportunity to do so. I guess when I don't have to get up, I don't mind it so much. It's just nice getting up as the Sun shines outside.

I got up this morning a little frightened again. In my dream I was at a table somewhere like a conference table. I had to leave. So I left. Then I don't remember all the details but I felt I had to go back and see Annie…because I had missed her. But it felt like I really wanted to be loved or affirmed somehow from her. when I couldn't find her, that's about the time I woke up a little scared.

I think it's difficult, if not impossible for us to live without love. Sometimes I wish I could be held like a baby in the comfort of a loved-one's arms without a care in the world…or as The Little Prince would say, without these "matters of consequences."

APRIL 25, 1999

(7:22 AM, SUNDAY MORNING)

It's the last Sunday before my trip to Europe. I'm still somewhat sleepy having just awoke.

I woke up with that frightened feeling again. Now I know exactly where that stemmed from. Perhaps it was due to the fact that it was colder last night. But really, as much as I don't enjoy admitting it, that frightened feeling stemmed from the fact that I need to be loved and held. Perhaps it's my pride.

Also, more directly, this feeling's been connected to my trip. I think deep inside, there is this tremendous hope that this other place, this other place that I had wondered about for so long may in fact be that place that I'd like to spend the rest (or most of) my life. Maybe it is the place where I'm accepted for who I am, accepted and appreciated that is.

Here in Los Angeles, in many ways, I suppose I'm accepted. There's a lot of freedom in terms of what you can do here. However, my soul feels lost and empty. It's not the kind of unpleasant feeling you get from say, a loss of a job, or perhaps even a broken heart. But it's more deeper and not so sharp. It's a dull sensation, and it's all around, all the time.

Yesterday, I heard that John Elway was retiring from football. One of his teammates said that his presence was always felt when he played. Now that he'll be gone, his absence will be felt.

It's kind of like that. Every team has a personality (so does every city). When a major player or landmark is gone, an era has changed. It's no longer the same place.

What I'm trying to say with all this is not too different from what mom and dad did by coming to the U.S. The economic opportunities were better here. I'm hoping the social and cultural economics are better for me in Europe...in Paris.

My fear is that I go there and realize that every place in the world is exactly like where I am right now—that I come back empty-handed without an olive branch between my beaks.

Home isn't so much a place, but a place in time.

Europe Travel Journal

(APRIL 27 – MAY 19, 1999)

8:18 a.m. on the train to Barcelona:

I was just reading "On Directing Film" by David Mamet. A thought was triggered when I read the sentence "When is the story over? When the hero gets it." (Boy, this is a rocky train ride!) Anyway, it reminded me of this trip. I had told Daron that "I had given up."— that I had stopped chasing after that illusive whale. Perhaps it was that I finally saw that this was an illusion, or I realized that the means I had weren't adequate for this conquest… this conquest that seemed to have had no specific end. Now I "get" it.

Now I'm not sure what the next step is. There are a couple of things that I'm thinking of. One is that I might like to go back to school and finish my Masters degree in Film or Animation. The other is perhaps to live in Paris (pending my approval of course). Or perhaps a combination of both. (Spain between Madrid and Barcelona does in fact look a lot like rural California.)

"…they are most happy who have no story to tell."

Now that my story seems to be over, will the next part of my life be another story? Or will it be quiet and happy?

I asked a question long ago, "Is it better to be sad and know the truth? Or, is it better to be happy and ignorant?" In some ways I feel I have the answer to that question now. The hero, protagonist, I found that there really seems to be no end for this quest. It all seems to be in the MEANS and not the END. "It ain't what you do it's the way that you do it."

Like Mamet's book refers to "reforming the large (superobjective) to better understand the small" and vice-versa. My life too, it seems, should follow this pattern.

I guess I could rephrase my original question this way now: Is it better to get what you know you want now? Or, is it better to wait and get what you'll think you'll want later?

I just had a "sandwich" on the train. The baguette was good but they don't put much in it—just one thin slice of meat. I have a feeling this whole trip was over rated.

MAY 2, 1999

BARCELONA 7:45 a.m., SUNDAY

I just made a call to TWA in regards to the schedule change. I won't be leaving Paris until the 18th of May. That makes my trip exactly 3 weeks. I did this to avoid going back to Madrid. It's that long train ride back. Also, it appears that the Eurail pass is initiated when you first get there, not when you start using the ticket! There was no way to spend a week in Paris without having to leave early for Madrid. Then I'd have to wait around a few extra days in Madrid. I enjoyed the city, but the time could be spent elsewhere.

I'll extend my stay in Italy where I'd have a chance to view more art and architecture. I shall have to start reading Italian soon.

Now onto the beginning of the journey: I haven't said much for Madrid partly because I only spent the two days there and partly because I was jet-lagged and in a daze. In fact, I woke up this morning in a beautiful hostel atop the city in Barcelona with a slight dizziness and nausea. Too many changes at once. I had a taste of my first home cooked meal in Barcelona. Food is good here. I had dinner with Juan and his wife and new baby of 10 days. What a fantastic apartment he has. Actually I think he owns it now. It's a 1920's Art Deco building on Paris Street. He's doing very well. He signed me a copy of his book on typography. We talked of days at Cal Poly.

I have yet to discover the rest of Barcelona, but physically as a city it's much less busy than MadriD—although women are quite beautiful in Madrid.

I had a chance to talk to a couple of fellow travelers here yesterday— Eric from Holland and Angela from Portugal. I talked to them on different times. Both had some reservations about the United States. Eric thought the U.S. should not be the world's police. If a country were to take such a position, they should first set an example. The U.S.

should be worthy before they can ask others to be the same. Angela, the industrial design student, didn't like the way Americans thought. They both thought that Americans were isolationists. Eric admired Holland's own economic prowess in that it was #7 on the global gross national product if I understood him correctly. He studied economics and spoke 4 or 5 languages. Not in so many words, but he did admire the U.S. economy.

Juan admired very much the Italians. He referred to them as a superior race than the Spanish, in particular for art and architecture. This is another reason why my schedule has changed slightly… to view more of Italy. I've had admired him for his thinking.

I've run across only one American so far. It was actually at a train station in Madrid. Her name is Ana. One American in 4 days. Very nice girl. She was studying Spanish in Madrid. She helped me with the train schedules. Very intelligent and attractive. Oh wait. I did meet 3 guys on the train to Barcelona. They were from the East Coast. One of them went to Penn. They were nice enough, but not too exciting.

May 7, 1999

8:25 p.m., FRIDAY

Now I just sat down on a nice train to Rome. I am in Nice. I stayed at a hostel atop, yet another beautiful mountaintop overlooking the Mediterranean Sea. I met a bunch of Canadians. They are a lot like Americans in behavior and thought, even though they didn't think so. If this wasn't true, why do most of them have some sort of Canadian flag or emblem sewn onto their backpacks and duffel bags? (By the way, I didn't take any pictures in Nice or Cannes because I didn't want to bother for just one night and two days.) In fact, I've heard one of them talk about a friend of theirs that had the Canadian Maple leaf tattooed on his shoulder along side "Made in Canada."

Luckily however, I befriended two of them, one of whom spoke French fluently. Their names were Nancy and Melanie. They both worked for the Phone Company. I met them at a bus stop going to the hostel. They both had groceries like myself because the hostel provided no food service, but had a kitchen. We all cooked together, a whole bunch of us. I bought some mussels in Cannes and boiled them in water with a bit of salt. Nice dinner. Later in the evening we (myself and the seven or eight Canadians) sat around a table with a few bottles of wine and conversed of drugs, philosophy, and the difference between Canada and America, and Canada and Europe, and Canada and the rest of the world.

By the way, this has been the cleanest train so far. Sleeping in a couchette isn't "all that" but it beats sleeping on a seat. Anyway, I spent the good part of the day in Cannes shopping and eating. I bought Laura Silverstein a toilet paper holder in Cannes. It's a 'gas.' She'll get a kick out of that since she collects toilet paper from around the world. My first test of speaking French happened here. You know, I can get quite fluent if I live in Paris. Had a nice time in Nice and Cannes. The film festival starts next week. They're preparing for it.

[-]

Okay, I didn't mention any experiences in Barcelona. There were plenty. I met some nice people. I have to say, the people influence me a lot on whether I want to visit their country. Now I don't care to go to Canada as much, but I'd be interested in visiting Slovakia. I'd be interested in Belgium, but not as much for Holland.

Here are the basic, face to face, superficial reasons, although reason enough: (1) Canada: too similar the U.S. and I don't care for the institutional attitudes as portrayed by those that I've met. This isn't unique to Canada. In fact, it's a lot like the United States. (2) Slovakia: I've met two very nice people from there. Zuzanna and Evelyna were quite down to earth, yet educated and worldly. (3) Belgium: I've met Bert who was very personable. He had a healthy attitude about life and people. He was open. (4) Holland: not interested because of the three people that I met all seem to be stuck on themselves. During the course of a conversation, one of them said that Europe had so many cultures within its geographical span and the United States had really, only one. Before I decided to tell him of the many subcultures within Los Angeles alone, I retaliated by saying that Europe had so many cultures because there were so many countries within such a small space. (5) Portugal: yes, I really like the people from there.

To touch upon a couple of experiences in Barcelona: One was the Picasso museum and the other was Lina. There were other activities but these two were noteworthy.

At the Picasso museum: I never, deep inside thought Picasso was really ever "all that." I've changed my mind in a big way. Although the famous ones were not in the Picasso Museum in Barcelona, I got a taste of his mastery. I viewed his early works and sketches, which were very nice. He is in fact very good at capturing light and shadow, feelings, etc. But it wasn't until I saw his Post-Blue Period works that I realized his true genius. To what extent his mastery ventured, I only began to see the entryway into an abyss. His works I believe now are far beyond the reaches of Dali, yet they are so very much in the present tense, here and now. His sketches of mainly women in their open sexuality are far removed from the taints of the mind. It's as if created these images directly from his "id" or whatever that core is called. Absolutely amazing.

The Strange Weather: It was the day before I departed for Nice from Barcelona. It was drizzly and wet. I was a tourist among the waterfront when upon a walk toward dry ground, a girl asks me for a cigarette... in Spanish of course. I replied that I had none, in what one MIGHT call Spanish. We conversed for a minute before deciding to get out of the rain. We are both laughing at our pathetic situation. She was a Russian girl visiting Barcelona on a visa. She spoke no Spanish except for a few words. I spoke even less Spanish. After intervals of about 30 minutes we were able to converse one message. As you may begin to see, at that rate, it would take the rest of the day to have a 10-minute conversation. So that is what we did. We spent the rest of the day together to finish our 10-minute conversation.

Here is what we said. While I was originally headed toward Nice, I decided that Nice could wait after our 2-day excursion to the Island of Mallorca. We decided to meet the next day at the harbor at 10:00 a.m.

In the meantime, that evening, we went back to my hostel to get something to eat. After that...

(Stopped writing to change trains)

(Okay, now I'm in one of the oldest trains in the system. There's lots of graffiti on the train, but the couchettes seem reasonable enough. I'm in bed now, top bunk of 3. There are 6 beds total in this cabin.)

...after that I proceeded to walk her back to the Metro station, when somehow in whatever language, we agreed to find a 'pension.' We found the closest thing, a hotel just down the street from the hostel. The rest they say, is a blur. Well, not really. Twice in the same night and a mutual shower. Fun. When the evening ended, I think we both knew somehow that the morning meeting to the Island of Mallorca was not going to happen.

In fact, when morning came, I went to the train station and prepared for my evening trip to Nice. Later that day I walked near the waterfront perhaps thinking that I might still see her standing around. At the same time, I'd avoid seeing her. I left for Nice at early evening wondering slightly, if she had waited for me there at the waterfront. I doubt it. She has my phone number in Los Angeles. She had no visa to visit the United States. I'd felt she wasn't interested in my "Master-Card" but perhaps she was interested in that Visa I could have given her. I never went to Mallorca to finish the 15-minute conversation.

Time to sleep.

MAY 8, 1999

SATURDAY, TOP BUNK OF THE HOSTEL IN ROME

Boy it was a pain in the ass getting here. I normally like a single ride on the Metro... then just walk to my final destination. However, when the train arrived in Rome, I spent at least 20 minutes looking for a locker to put away my luggage. I finally found them. But when I put my suitcase in it, it locked up and shut off an entire section of these electronic lockers, rendering them useless. Worse yet, I couldn't get it back out. Luckily, the man in charge of those lockers was nearby. I decided to take the extra 50 pounds to the hostel. I read ahead of time that this location had lockers.

MAY 10, 1999

MONDAY, ON THE TRAIN TO FLORENCE 10:00 a.m.

My how time seems to be flying. Yet, I feel like I've been on my trip awhile. The thing about travelling is that while many say it broadens one's horizons, I think what happens is that our horizon stays the same width and more information is packed within this space. So that what seems large and important, seems smaller and trivial. The world gets more localized. The magical other place is demystified into an experience of the senses. The imagined becomes real. And the real is never as colorful as the imagined. Everything wonderful seems to be within.

When two people are in a passionate love affair, no... better yet, when one takes it to understand it as a one-night affair and the other understands it as a serious love affair, who is right? Most often, the one that thinks of it as a one-night fling will tell the other that there was no more to it than that. The one that thought of it as a serious love affair is left in a state of confusion and at a loss. Perhaps it is the exception in love affairs that both must feel and more importantly, believe in the love. I'm not sure.

But in the case of parent-child love, the love we feel must be as great or even greater, yet the child is unaware. Again, the old question, "If a tree fell in a forest and no one was there to hear (or witness) it, then did the tree fall?" There's two ways to answer this. One is YES, because the condition of the situation in the question was that the tree fell, regardless. It's already defined in the question. Two is also YES if you choose to believe it as perhaps in the case of love. Okay, there is a third answer NO. It is possible in the supposition that all reality, the only realm of truth, is in the physical senses. Again, everything seems to be within and subjective.

Yet the more the world is demystified the more safety one has to believe in one's OWN truth, realities, dreams and aspirations that he has had for so long internally, slowly burning with signs of a personal and unique roadmap unlike any other.

To believe in one's own roadmap must take great courage for those who are not so sure. When we grow into adulthood and are aware of our own consciousness and nakedness, are we not afraid?—Because the journey now is all solo and very conscious.

And what of those that never take that road? Or those that take it very late? Does anyone actually complete them? I suppose if life indeed is a journey and not a destination, it must be better to start late than never start at all. I am sad.

[later]

I did not want to leave Rome but the journey continues. It was not the bricks in the Coliseum or the fountains or hundreds of other monuments that tugged at my heart, but a beautiful young woman that I had spent a good two days with. Vanessa, the Belgium-born Italian girl whose native tongue was French with fluency in Italian and fair English, and I hopped from one monument to another. We communicated pretty well with mostly English and occasional French. She was a lovely girl—kind of plain from a distance, but graceful and gentle up close. Hazel eyes and chestnut-brown hair, she was well filled-out and not too thin like the French and American ideal. She was somewhat of a cross between Sophia Loren and the girl from the Tango Scene in "Scent of a Woman." I will send her a copy of the movie.

[later]

The Italian countryside is nice, much like Northern California. The train ride is about two hours or so to Florence (Firenze). I am constantly interchanging words from different languages… (hold on, I actually ran out of ink!) …thinking that people will understand. I knew so little Spanish but when I got to Nice, I found myself saying "Hola" and "Gracias." The word "Hola" has become dear to me now because that's one of the first words that I've used upon landing in Europe. And what was once a phonetic sound has became an actual word to covey messages and acknowledge one another. Now when I meet people, I enjoy saying "Hola." When I say goodbye, I like "Ciao."

MAY 12, 1999

WEDNESDAY 5:18 p.m. TRAIN STATION, FLORENCE

It's about 2 ½ hours before I depart for Paris. I spent 2 nights in Florence, but a day in Venice. I met 2 Americans from the University of Michigan (Ann Arbor I believe) on the way to the city by the water. We had a great time. The three of us, Jeannie, Katie, and I took a ride on the Gondola through a picturesque surrounding of brick, boats, and murky water. I asked the Gondola Operator to sing a song for us. But he thought I should sing instead. He did whistle however. Lunch was spent at a café overlooking the water. Everyone has a cellular phone. Even our Gondola Operator was talking on one while navigating through the tiny canals. He was pretty friendly.

Speaking of service people, the public interface i.e. salespeople, attendants, etc., are not always friendly. The last example was about an hour ago when I ordered a couple of slices of pizza. I'd asked for a fork and knife. He replied that he only had a knife. He gave me the knife, which I placed on the tray, but could not really use without a fork. Then the older one, perhaps the father, grunted a few words to the younger one. I figured he was complaining about me and those "damn tourists" But it wasn't until a couple of the Italian women looked over knowingly that I realized he was saying something worse. I searched my memory banks to retrieve the Stella Adler Academy of Acting class techniques. In my best Italian look of disgust, I glared at him. He turned away in complete humiliation and shame thinking perhaps that I knew all along what he was talking about. Throughout my meal he kept looking over at me while trying not to be noticed. His face was red with an expression of "Oh my God, I'm found-out."

There is an air of Anti-American sentiment here in general. In Venice, I saw a poster of an anti-NATO graffiti. Besides the poster there is nothing explicit, but really just a strong undertone. Perhaps it is because Florence and Venice are closer to the Kosovo-Yugo disturbance than Rome. Or perhaps they just don't like Americans.

Florence is beautiful from a distance, but a little grungy up close. Frankly, it will be good to leave Florence. Public service is never great, I suppose, in any country. But Italy, in particular Florence, needs help most.

MAY 18, 1999

TUESDAY 10:50 a.m. CHARLES DE GAULLE AIRPORT, PARIS

One week had passed since my stay in Paris began. One of the girls I met, Kristine from Switzerland, when asked if travel broadens one's horizon, she replied that if you're open to meeting people, open to understanding the different cultures, then your horizon will in fact grow, but otherwise it will probably not. She's one of the smartest 16 year-olds I've met... One of the smartest people I've met. I hope she keeps in touch.

Why are we open to some things and not others? There must be something inside, some curiosity, some flavors we have smelt, or a clue to a road map of our personhood to drive these doors open to the out-side. I was happy to be in Paris.

6:00 p.m. PARIS TIME. EN ROUTE TO NYC on TWA #942

Just watched "You've Got Mail." There's probably another couple of hours before landing. I've been thinking about Vanessa. In my wild imagination I wished so dearly that she was perhaps thinking about me—that perhaps when I get back to L.A., I will continue to write let-ters—that perhaps we'd both move to Paris as our common ground.

I've heard of those people who've had a near-death experience. They saw themselves rising out of their bodies and going toward a tunnel of light. They described it as this wonderful place. When, however, they had to return to their lives because it wasn't "their time," they awoke in an uncontrollable sob. They did not want to return.

The place I went physically was Europe. When the physical geog-raphy is changed, the inner geographer travels too. In fact, it was the inner traveler that kept me in the state of wanting to stay in this place, THIS OTHER PLACE! And when I began to realize the end of my stay at this other place, I just wanted to sob uncontrollably, like being kicked out of Eden.

2:09 p.m. EASTERN TIME, JFK AIRPORT

I'm tired but comfortable. I don't have to be as aware as I would be in a foreign country. Everything is in English… though in Paris, I didn't feel too lost. It did not feel like a foreign city. It felt like a do-mestic city and a lot of people happen to be speaking French.

Back Home

JUNE 15, 1999

(9:32 AM, TUESDAY)

I've been back from Europe for about a month now. And Europe has begun to fade into a memory. It was in Barcelona, at the museum, that I had returned to thoughts of architecture. And throughout the rest of my trip that thought kept reoccurring. Since my trip, I had registered for the GRE as well as registered for the GRE class. I remembered how difficult and tricky those questions on the test could be. I am now in prep mode for architecture school, including research on the schools themselves. So far: UCLA, Rice, Princeton, Harvard, U of Virginia, and U of Washington.

It's as though I'm picking up my life where I left off three years ago. I've registered for the rowing class and going back into architecture. That's also when I was last dating someone (besides Anita) with more of a heart's investment. My heart was with Audrey, but of course we were never really "dating."

I'm more comfortable being back from my trip now. I had mentioned that I wanted to sob uncontrollably as I was leaving Europe. But I believe that I am now somehow preparing in whatever metaphysical means to journey back into the place that I had only seen from my heart's eye, like looking through a glass into paradise or Eden, untouchable, yet real.

SEPTEMBER 5, 1999

(9:20 AM, SUNDAY)

What a frightening nightmare.

There was this mirror in front of me.

I looked into it. In one corner, I thought I saw something. So I turned around and there was this being, like death. It didn't look like, but it *felt* like, that being in the film with Donald Sutherland. The movie with the "red" motif throughout…[*Don't Look Now*]

—except that my being was all in black. It was like seeing The Grim Reaper.

OCTOBER 12, 1999

(9:30 PM, TUESDAY EVENING)

Sometimes (as I have read past entries) I see that a lot of what I say in here aren't necessarily "right on." I mean, I try to be. But when I look back, the things I say or express are oftentimes masks for how I really feel or think. And I wonder how long in my lifetime it will take to be really that honest.

I am definitely sincere, but it is shrouded by ignorance I can only see after some time has gone by, or maybe not even ignorance, but a youth's arrogance.

I took some sleeping pills. That's keeping me from thinking too much.

I've had a couple of dreams lately that were pretty vivid. I'll tape-in the printed copies later. Bur one was most incredibly wonderful. Yes, the one with water and people everywhere. The other was quite scary. It was in the multi-story building. And all I really remember is a set of winding (marble) stairs that I was going up and down in. And near the center was the sort of creature that was supposed to represent death or something. I only saw the head. I also remember carrying a baby. Yes, it was mine and this girl's. I think it was Rochelle, not sure. I remember in the dream that this place was a morgue or something similar. Eventually, I decided to leave the place altogether, with baby and Rochelle. Baby was not attractive. But it did feel good to be leaving that place.

Woke up.

[later]

Also what I notice about my writing is that they all seem to be very opinionated or have some sort of predictive nature about it. By predictive, I mean that I'm trying to predict things: How I feel about things or others. Yet, looking back, I really didn't know what I was talking about.

I think I was more afraid of *not knowing* than knowing something bad. I think what I just said is monumental! This has been a source for so much trouble for me.

Blessed my creative mind! When I didn't know the answer to something, I often made up something just to ease the mental pain of not knowing.

Wow, from religion to relationships to career—this makes a lot of sense. And I wonder now about how little faith I had (have). And perhaps I can believe in, or at least wait for the unknown to resolve itself.

OCTOBER 13, 1999

(10:43 PM, WEDNESDAY EVENING)

Note to self: remember to tape in here also: "the connection dream" (in email somewhere)

OCTOBER 17, 1999

(7:36 AM, SUNDAY)

I've had this journal open for the past 5 to 10 minutes. I have a lot on my mind. Yet they really are not thoughts of burden. They are thoughts about my career and my life.

As I prepare myself for graduate school, I begin to see what might make me happy, content, and fulfilled. And I must and do wonder if producing films will do that for me. It's hard to say.

As strange as it sounds, while that may be in my future, the road immediately ahead of me indicates otherwise. I see myself joining an actors' group or theatre group. In the meantime, I can see my graphic design work slowing down to allow for these changes. It's quite difficult to understand the inklings of the voices inside, but I think if I'm still enough and listen very carefully I can hear it.

One thing I'll always remember when I was with Catherine is that she said, "Nothing forced is ever beautiful."

It feels like the next step should be a smaller one. And it almost feels like grad school will put that gradual and natural growth on hold or displaced.

I went to a showing of a Korean film at UCLA yesterday. I told David's friend Chris about my plans for applying to UCLA's producer's program and that perhaps I should apply to a "back up" school. He said just apply again the next year. In the meantime, do what you should be doing...i.e. growing in and doing what you are interested in.

That made so much sense to me.

It had made me think that perhaps the graduate education was perceived in my mind as a material possession—and really, material possessions have their place, but no in the context of my life.

NOVEMBER 15, 1999

(NOVEMBER 16, 1999 MONDAY EVENING/TUESDAY

MORNING 12:21 AM)

It's the night before Brian leaves for Hawaii. I hope he will be happy there.

It's amazing how unpredictable my life is from month to month—especially as I read past journal entries.

(why is it that when I try to go to sleep, I can't. And when I try to stay awake, I want to fall asleep?)

What's on my mind now is Boston. Perhaps in a couple of weeks I will visit the city with the standby ticket. I've heard such wonderful things about the town.

Quite frankly, I'm tired of moving around. And yet, I'm seeking... though not too actively.

I've been in L.A. for 4 years and the friends that I have are still the friends I've had before I moved here.

I feel like I'm living in a town full of self-centered 'retards.' It's not nourishing me in ways, other than food (which I have no complaints of). I'm not connecting here. It's not (perhaps) that people don't want to connect. I think people are more concerned with immediate needs: food, sex, wealth, and perhaps a few other material things.

I really want to like L.A. And I've always defended it. But now I'm feeling a bit embittered by it all. People are retarded here, like living with 10 million Neanderthals. Ok, so I'm exaggerating to point out the distaste in my mouth. But there's some truth in that.

DECEMBER 17, 1999 [EMAIL TO DARON]

Subject: The most wonderful dream

I think last night, my head must have been full of things that I was unaware of.

As I recall parts of, what I'd call, the best dream in my life, I remember this large 2 or 3 story white Victorian house with large windows. In this house is a family, perhaps Hispanic. It's a very happy family. They show me around their house in a small boat, sort of like that one at "It's a Small World" at Disneyland. And outside the house, I can see water everywhere. On one side of the house is a carnival with fireworks, a glow of a festival, and lots of lights. The other side is a deep ocean, yet to be seen by morning. The family invites me to eat with them. The father calls the son downstairs to eat. The little boat tours around from inside the house showing the view of the outside. The center of the house comprise of the stairwell and kitchen.

Another part of the dream is that I'm on a different boat, a large yacht. It's as if the Pacific Ocean and the Mediterranean were next to each other. I'm floating by in this incredibly aqua-turquoise colored water. The surrounding area is rocky. There are some friends with me. They ask me to swim in the water. I dive head in. Couple of the girls turn out to be Mermaids. At first it seemed a little frightening because of the fishy tails. But I knew it was fine when they swam back to the boat when they were done swimming. After swimming, I get back in the boat. We cruise along the peninsula of what might be Palos Verdes.

This segues into another water area: The Mediterranean. Now I'm in a place like Venice. There are old buildings everywhere surrounded by this water. The buildings have warmth to them because there are people living in them—lots of people. Now I'm in a smaller boat, perhaps a gondola or the like. As a few of us move along the waterways, I'm invited to go to a party. When I tell them I have to finish doing some work they insist that I have time to do it later. I go to the party. When I get there it's not just a party. There are several parties to choose from. One is quiet and friendly, sitting under some wispy trees, talking, perhaps with a fire. Another is just a door and I see people coming in and out from it. But I don't think anyone is supposed to know about that one. The third one is the one I ended up going. It's a large dance/ballroom. The music is contemporary. I am with these friends. We form a line of two to do a "dance-through." One side women; the other side men. The guys are laughing and joking about who's going to standing facing one of the girls.

It seems the day of this event-period was nearly done and I began collecting my things to go home. I proceeded to walk with my arm full of my clothes. I know. I was headed back to the yacht. (Now that I think of it, it wasn't a sailing yacht. It was a motor yacht). Anyway, I'm heading that way when a nice girl invites me to dinner at this large table of people. I get to this restaurant with large windows with a view of the harbor of small boats. The table is long. There are two or three empty seats in the middle. The girl tells me that I should sit there. To my right are four or five more girls. They are all pretty and friendly. They are glad to see me and tells me so. A man is sitting to the left of me. He says something like "I haven't seen people so polite since England."

Then I woke up.

DECEMBER 28, 1999

(7:47 AM)

The following 12-week period consists of writings called the "Morning Pages." It is intended to be used with the book "The Artist's Way at Work." I am to write 3 pages every morning. (just sounds like my "normal" journal writing except that I do it every day, rather than whenever I feel like it)

[later]

There are several things going on right now. First, I am designing a logo for John Kiranian called "Soapz." It's not a great name. It has to be used with care so that it doesn't sound cheap.

I feel a little rushed, as I write this because I feel I have too much to do as it is. But it is nice to get up knowing I don't owe a big part of my life to someone else, namely a job.

A thought just occurred to me. As I wait for my admissions notice from UCLA and Directors' Guild, the fastest way to success would be to start my own design company. But then again, I thought about the Masters degree, which I'd like to finish.

It seems all very confusing trying to figure out how I will go about reaching where I want to be. Perhaps I'm well on my way. When I tell people that I've applied to the producer's program, lots of them (including Daron and Adam) think I should be pursuing Directing instead. Initially I think that that's true. But when I think about it, producing is very exciting as well. I find it important that I am the initiator and creator of a project—that I make it come to life from near nothing to something tangible. I think it also has to do with the "material" or "object" side of me. There was something I noticed about myself in the way I relate to jobs, people, and everything else. It helps me to understand when I can place the relational subject, be it people, places, or jobs, into a visual and at least quasi-tangible object.

I've been thinking about Annie a lot lately—and for good reason. I've asked her out on a date. Initially, I was very attracted to her. Then I had my reservations. Besides the obvious fact that we work together, she had some "Hollywood-style anything to get to the top" behavior. That turned me off for a while. But over the year, I've seen her sweet side too. And to her credit, she's always treated me nice and with respect. Now that she's leaving to work for YBC, that door just got a little wider—and she's looking much prettier.

There is something about change that makes us get a haircut. And then there are those changes that make us buy a new car.

I think I understand why a car *really* is a status symbol. Besides the obvious money factor, a car is about attitude. A car is closely linked to one's career. Sometimes we buy cars to make that leap of faith into the next career realm when we've outgrown the present situation. Logistical issues aside (preparing for school), I've been thinking of upgrading my BMW to the newer model.

DECEMBER 29, 1999

(8:26 AM, WEDNESDAY)

As I was waking up, I remember thinking the word "friendship" just before I opened my eyes. When I opened them the word "love" came out of my mouth. Of course, what I was thinking about was Annie.

I hope something works out, although I think about keeping some distance as not to get too hopeful. I always feel like I have so much to do. And I feel like I can't do them *all* well. For instance, the video project.

—you know, I really don't feel much like writing in here.

I have to rearrange the apartment so that the office is back to normal.

My mind wanders off to Brian starting his Chiropractic school in the fall. He apparently will get his own place. He won't be working, but he'll be going to school full time and living on his own. The money will be provided by Dad so he can concentrate on his coursework. I'm a little (not a lot) disappointed that I never had that kind of a chance, even when I asked for it.

Life has its "own" way.

Trey is back from Connecticut. He seems to be doing fine.

DECEMBER 30, 1999

(6:08 PM, THURSDAY)

Okay, it's not quite morning, but I thought I'd write down a few notes. I'm exhausted from not getting enough sleep last night—2 hours to be exact.

I ended up shooting video at Trey's until around 9:30 PM—not that late, but I had to go back a second time when I forgot the battery chargers.

Got up at 4 AM for the airport shuttle after going to bed at 2:00 AM from packing. What's on my mind right now? Not much. Too tired. I just want to sleep.

The flight over here to Vegas was pretty spectacular. Morning sunset from a mile above the ground and clouds was amazing in its shades of orange and reds.

Now I'm thinking about work at Vanguard Advertising. It's not all that terrible. But I do picture myself in an environment more conducive to vision and inspiration. The money is good. So, I'll stay, probably, until I find out some answers about school/Directors' Guild.

One thing this school situation brings up is how it relates to Annie. If I'm in school for a couple of years, will she still want to date me? I'm not sure if perhaps she's going to want someone already "in place" of success—you know, someone who's already got himself established. My best hope is that we go out and things work out, even when I'm in school.

So, Trey is out from Connecticut. He's thinking of buying a 5500 square feet house there, 3 or 4 stories. I believe his parents are helping him out with this. I wouldn't mind having a house again. I was always afraid that I'd end up moving. It's as if I'm putting off a lot of things because I'm waiting on something else. I'm sure a big reason for this is that if I commit to something like a house or even a wife/girl, then I may be closing off the doors to the bigger picture. It's about timing. I need to build the foundation first, but it seems at times that it's taking much too long—do I wait for the concrete of the foundation to dry, or do I continue? I'm waiting for it to dry. Admittedly, I had been confused about the "house of my life" blueprints.

2000 The Escape Plan

JANUARY 1, 2000

(9:28 AM, SATURDAY)

Oops. I forgot to write an entry for yesterday. I was busy getting food and alcohol.

The party was reasonably successful. Slow at first. Harry has changed a lot since I knew him at first. He's now (mostly) openly gay, whereas before, as I see it now, he used to go to church to (probably) repent his feelings and inklings. I think he used to live a secret life.

What's my secret life? I've been thinking about one thing: *Paris*. This defies all logic and rational thinking. I cannot explain my desire to be there and perhaps live there. There is no reason other than the fact that it weaves through my thoughts every now and then. I was supposed to go to Paris for New Year's but I cancelled it for a couple of reasons. One, it's expensive, taking so much time off and not making money. Two, because things didn't work out between Rochelle and myself, I must have thought that the real reason I planned my trip to Paris was because we talked about going together. And now I realize I wanted to go there regardless. But perhaps this is what I wanted to find out by staying here. I was testing myself. I remember in April, when I was there at the Eiffel Tower, I saw the sign counting down the days 'til the new 2000 year, and wishing somehow I could be back for that party.

Now I must wonder which desires truly belong to me and which belong to a set of rules that can program (brainwash?) anyone's mind. I can't help but think of the "Truman Show."

JANUARY 2, 2000

(10:15 AM, SUNDAY)

I have just a moment before Harry and I have to meet Bill for breakfast.

I "went out" last night. Harry went to the Gypsy, his gay club. I went to C2K at the Venetian. The lines were so long that I ended up not going at all. I did win some cash at Video Poker though.

I wonder how Bill's doing these days. I guess I'll find out in an hour or so. I wonder if marriage was all that he thought it'd be.

I don't feel I have much to talk about. I just keep thinking of where I want to take Annie for our first date. Descanso Gardens would be nice, I think. I've never taken anyone to a place like that for a date. I'll ask her what she thinks. I hope she's looking forward to this as much as I am.

…Harry's ready to go. Bye for now.

JANUARY 3, 2000

(MONDAY)

Ah ha! Just as I suspected, the New Year is exactly like the old year in terms of all that Y2K crap—which goes to show you that people are purposely on the lookout for problems, situations, etc. to give themselves some meaning. But again, it's the same story. People are longing to unite, to fight for a common cause, to bring themselves together. Yet when there is not an apparent cause, people seem to generate a "false" one.

Until such a cause appears, everything seems suspect: religion, politics, money…boiling down to the natural urges to mate and bare children; to conquer and win, like the spreading of a disease or a growth of biological cells.

This sort of brings it to a personal level now. My "high" aspirations of becoming someone important, I wonder, is being faded out for the natural urges to mate and bare offspring. Life has its own timing, and when it calls, there is nothing to do except beckon that call. "You don't have to scream at a rose for it to bloom" –Someone I can't remember.

Oh, is *that* what' I'm getting at? Please excuse myself for being so corny and clichéd. But that is what seems to be happening. Gee whiz, golly, I'm blooming. Seems kind of late.

[later]

You know, when I used to look for girls to date, I wanted someone, not too high-a-profile in monetary or sociological terms because I liked or perhaps wanted someone I can "struggle" with *together*. But I think it's a lot like what I said about people creating a false cause to have meaning in their lives. But with Annie, I'm not looking for that cause. She treats me nice and with respect—and that counts a lot in my book now. Although I'd always been attracted to her, I think I was blind. She's moving up in the world. She's got great connections. She's sociable, pretty, tall and elegant. And…she likes me. She sees something in me, like a potential of some sort. I like that.

JANUARY 5, 2000

(9:05 AM, WEDNESDAY)

My mind is scattered and frantic right now. I'm thinking of a zillion things I must get done. Yet when I think about it, I have ample time to do them all.

I think the combination of reading the book and doing these "morning pages" are actually helping my attitude. I am slowly becoming more positive in myself and my behavior, going from "I have a great idea" and losing steam to "I have a great idea and this is who I should call to get things done."

I have to admit something here. I've been thinking about Annie more than I'd like to admit. As I was close to waking up this morning, she was in my dream. And as I got up, I said to myself that if she was in my dream, then she was probably thinking (or dreaming) of me too.

I wish all the fears would go away about loving someone—and perhaps they will.

[later]

Too many things. I shall sit down and plan it out. I think it's because I think to myself, "I have this week off and it's the only full week I have off for a long time to come. So I better get as much done as possible." But I think I should relax and get a few key things done then relax some more.

[later]

Renée's birthday is coming up. Her birthday party is in two weeks. Adam said Linda will be there. Nice girl.

[later]

I think part of my fears for getting involved with Annie is/was that perhaps I'd have to come out into the open where I can be seen, "to be in the center of it all and not bat an eye." But I wonder perhaps that this is what I need. Yes, she has that "Hollywood-ness" to her, but she does have a good attitude.

JANUARY 6, 2000

(8:40 AM, THURSDAY)

I got to get this place cleaned up and organized today! It feels like this monumental task—although if I think about it, I should be able to get it done by noon. Perhaps I shall have to budget out my time. 9-11:30: clean up; 12:00: lunch with Carrie.

I'm a little sad this morning. I was very happy yesterday. I went out to El Mirage, the dry lake bed to scout out a shooting location. It was beautiful out there.

I am most happy when my world is full of possibilities and I'm curious about much. I am most sad when my world is closed off and there is no magical sense of wonder, and all jobs seem to lead to a mechanical duty. Do I ask for too much?

I think sometimes I'm just a little boy. Perhaps that is my fascination with The Little Prince.

The stock market is going bonkers. Oracle went from 117 to 101 in the last few days. Ouch!

I hope something wonderful happens this year.

Why do I have so much to do? Or why do I think I have so much to do? I need to massively simplify some things—throw away things I don't need. Let's empty out the trash of my mind!

JANUARY 7, 2000

(9:41 AM, FRIDAY)

Had a drink with Gertrude last night. She looked good. I'm having her and Sheena over for dinner on Sunday. Perhaps I should have Alex over too. Or Trey. Hmm.

I've been debating whether to take French class or not. It starts tomorrow. I think I will. It seems my life will get quite busy again. Hopefully I can balance it out. My social life is starting to pick up too.

My mind is a blank for something to write. My mind is elsewhere. I need to clean up before people come over tonight.

JANUARY 9, 2000

(SUNDAY)

Yesterday, the Actor Gil Angelo called me at 6:00 PM to say he won't make it. Fucker! I set up the entire shoot, fog machine and all, and he decided not to show up.

Had a tough time sleeping last night. I kept rolling around and my mind would not rest. Yes, I ate a little too much, but as I recall, I think my mind was on Annie and Linda. Perhaps subconsciously, I'm in turmoil over whom to pick. And the silly thing is, is that I haven't officially been out with either one of them. If I never met either one and met them just recently, I might go with Linda. But that is not the case. I've got to know Annie somewhat over the year. And yes, she has some annoying traits but I've come to appreciate her and her good attributes as well. Linda, I don't know that well, but I have a lot of respect for Adam and Renée's opinions. Renée at least thinks the world of her. I think Adam likes her too but he probably sees a few more faults than Renée does. It should be interesting next weekend when I'll see Linda at Renée's birthday party and Annie (presumably) on our first official date.

[later]

Sheena and Gertrude are coming over for dinner tonight. They're bringing Pictionary. That should be fun. They invited me over several times, one of which I was able to attend for dinner. They're great people. Trey couldn't make it. He started getting his annual cold and flu symptoms. It would be nice to invite someone tonight that wasn't a couple. Maybe I'll ask my neighbor Pam. She's actually a couple too. Come to think of it, there aren't too many single persons I know.

JANUARY 11, 2000

(6:05 AM, TUESDAY)

Annie's birthday. I didn't sleep too well. I've been thinking about Annie all night. I said to myself yesterday that I'd need a miracle for something here to work. Honestly, I've been a little scared myself. She wanted to postpone the date and thought we should talk about this first. Agreed. I think she wants to really date me but perhaps is looking for a more secure connection. Same here. We really need to talk.

It seems as though I've been having a battle of brain vs. heart. Freud says, use the mind for the little decisions and the heart for the larger decisions. That's always been my conflict. And as I think about the past experiences…Trina: I think she wanted to make sure that I did in fact love her (she didn't have a nice way of enquiring).

(9:25 PM)

I'm tired.

JANUARY 12, 2000

(5:23 AM, WEDNESDAY)

Too much on my mind to even sleep. When a child is very young he tries to hide the world by covering his eyes with his hands. The world seems to turn dark and it seems to go away. It occurred to me. I think I've been doing a lot of that through my adult life. For example, in love relationships, I feel love or hate or anger and I convince myself that it's okay to be a certain way. All the while the other party is looking at me closing my eyes and looking foolish.

I think the best philosophy to live by is the one without it.

It's not because it's easier, but because it's more true. In fact, it's more difficult to live this way because it is living by faith; living beyond one's (dare I say) imagination; it's just "being." Pureness.

Love relationships are so difficult for me; at least for one of the reasons, the example of the child covering his eyes to make the world go away. Just because I love someone doesn't make it okay to not express that love in some tangible way.

I think part of the reason why modern dating rituals consist of so much game playing is (besides fear of rejection) because we do know on a deeper level what we're looking for. It's a matter of self resolve to match and balance the world of desire and passion with intellect, looks, money, family and everything else. It's about knowing the limits as much as the possibilities and potential. In that way, I think it's better to be wise than to learn from another experience—the very similar experience has already been made by someone else.

What's amazing to me is to learn how much my so-called 'uneducated' parents really know about the world. Another thing is to see how well-off financially my parents are given the adversarial and humbling position from which they started.

Getting back to the wise, I couldn't sleep because I was thinking of Annie. I felt my "heart" was with her while my "wisdom" was with Linda. My "heart" woke me up. My heart seems to always speak to me in my sleep. Yet when I'm awake, it's my mind and wisdom that speak.

I must understand what is meant by "heart." Freud: "in small matters, use your mind. In large matters, use your heart." I understand the statement. I have difficulty understanding three of the words in that sentence: 1) heart 2) small 3) large.

Small and large are relative terms to be determined on an individual level subject to what he's capable of handling and to what capacity it has meaning for his life. The word "heart" puzzles me. It is used in so many ways. We all seem to agree on its meaning, and yet it's still so vague. What does it mean to follow your heart? And what does it mean to have heart? "She followed her heart, but forgot to turn off the oven when she left." –Me

JANUARY 13, 2000

(7:45 AM)

At the beach: Coincidence? Hmm. I walked toward the water to sip my apple cider. What do I see? Somebody scribed a double heart (a heart within a heart) about 6 feet in front of me. "I followed my heart and it led me to the beach." I haven't been here in a while. It's one of my sacred grounds, especially very early in the morning. I seem to come here whenever I have troubles with my heart. It's a place to replenish what I lost.

I think I tend to jump the gun during initial relationships. But I think with the right person, that is minimized and there is more room for mistakes overall.

My heart has been hurt. It takes me to strange and volatile places. I wonder, that is, if I still believe in the saying, "follow your heart" it's because my heart is teaching without a doubt where I stand—to know fully the deepest secrets that would have never emerged—to live that deeply—and ultimately to love that deeply. "How can you know the secrets of your heart without breaking it open?" –K.G.

Lots of people have small or no hearts. They scramble and scrounge for whatever little they can get their hands on.

Anyway, my shadow's getting shorter here which means the early morning quiet is dissipating.

MARCH 5, 2000

(10:21 PM, SUNDAY NIGHT)

It's been about 1 month since I opened up my own shop—had one job for logo and stationary, a small web banner ad, and a finish of a web design for ReelStock. I've been taking more Pepcid A.C. tablets to reduce the acid in my stomach. I suppose it's expected having started my own business.

[later]

Just read a few of the past entries for this year. It's really funny to see how things change. It's hard to believe that, that whole thing with Annie was only barely two months ago. It seems so long ago. Yet, other events, like my trip to Vegas doesn't seem that long ago at all.

As I read over some of the old Annie notes, I laugh. To think that that's how I thought of her two months ago. And only about 5-6 weeks ago, I was cursing her for having played me.

B I T C H !

She will *never* get another chance. She overvalues herself like cheap stock for her fragile ego. She's a coward like so many people. No woman of mine should lack courage or grace. She has neither.

I need to stop forgiving people for having punished me—as if it were an invitation to do more damage. If it should happen, I'll wait for them to ask for forgiveness.

MARCH 18, 2000

(MARCH 19, 2000 SATUDAY EVENING/MORNING 12:49 AM)

Hey two movies in one week. Haven't done that in awhile. It's fun going to the movies. I have to go alone sometimes because some of my "theatre" snobs can't extract content from context, or vice versa.

I'm a little tired now. Just saw "Pitch Black" and was quite bored. Yesterday I saw "Ninth Gate" and that was much better. Hollywood greed + Screenwriting 101 = Pitch Black.

Business is starting to pick up. Monday, I have a meeting with Timothy and Cathleen of the Hollywood Film School. I'm already doing an ad, flyer and brochure for them. Now I'll meet with them for an ad campaign.

I'll meet with Jeri next Tuesday. This is kind of cool—getting work without having to have done a single cold call or run or mail an ad.

Annie called me last Sunday at work. I thought it was strange that she would call me there on a Sunday. I'm always questioning people's motives and I wonder why she'd call me at work on a Sunday, and then actually be able to reach me. There's something too much of a coincidence there—nothing to worry about. I just thought it was odd. She apologized for not having called in awhile. But it seems like she just wanted the air to clear.

Lately, I've been sort of resigned from many things like dating, career (though not as much as dating), and perhaps life in general. For example, on this Saturday Night: Even less than a year ago, I might have felt I had to be doing something. Lately I began to think, "what is telling me that I have to do that?"

I imagined myself like I was in Madrid. I didn't speak Spanish. So, what I needed to do was to create my own entertainment and adventures. Find things that I find interesting or entertaining. Fact is, I didn't ever really think going to a bar was that entertaining. As I look at it now, they're neither hardcore enough nor friendly enough. It's nice to get a drink sometimes and relax. But really, what a waste of time and money. The bars are often filled with people who don't want to be alone. But I guess it is better to be alone together.

It's as if there is this collective and communal consciousness. Perhaps it is called society. And there is this unstated but lurking pressure of influence that says one has to be "in" with the collective in order to be validated and accounted for.

I guess what's amazing to myself is that I am feeling less and less of a need to be in the "heart" of it all—because in this heart of the collective is not where mine own lives. And while it is nice to know for a brief moment that I am a part of a larger whole, it's really better to know that I am a complete "one" on my own right. And that relaxes me amidst all the business and creative activities that are going on right now.

MARCH 19, 2000

(MARCH 20, 2000 SUNDAY EVENING/MORNING 12:56 AM)

Julia and Dina were just over here to hang out.

I noticed something. Perhaps it is only with women, but I think I've become quite shy again—or perhaps I never left the shyness to begin with.

I noticed myself constantly apologizing for so many things. I kept explaining things over. Like when I was showing the Los Angeles Choir videos at the Music Center, I would say that we'd sound better if it weren't for the audio.

I don't think I do that with men.

[later]

Mina called today. I hadn't mentioned her in here so far. I think what I need most in my life is meaning. And sometimes I wonder if I need meaning more than I need love.

But see, there's something meaningful *and* romantic with Mina's situation. How often is it that you meet someone at a place like the Eiffel Tower, to think you'd never see again, but to find you see her again a few days later at the Louvre, then lose sight of her without having exchanged contact info, then see her again the day before I leave Paris?

And really, I find it difficult to believe that we have actually kept in touch. Now, I may end up marrying her. The only person I told was Mick. He's close but not in the "inner-inner" circle. Not to diminish his friendship in any way. In fact, I tell him things because he seems to listen without being too judgmental or critical. I may visit her sometime soon in Azerbaijan.

MARCH 20, 2000

(MARCH 21, 2000 MONDAY EVENING 12:06 AM)

Been back from seeing a movie called "My Dog Skip"—cute and sweet. Makes one think about having a dog. Perhaps toward the end of the year after the business starts rolling, I shall get one.

I'm a little tired.

I met with Timothy and Cathleen of the Hollywood Film School to discuss the ad campaign for the film school.

I'm very lonely.

Seeing the movie reminds me of my own scattered childhood. There were many good parts like catching dragonflies and frogs, or tasting snow on the tongue as it fell from the sky. Riding sleds on the frozen rice patties were really cool. But people…people are just cruel. They don't fulfill me. And if one more person suggests a relationship with God, I'm going to strangle them. "Let go, and let God."—like a fucking recipe book or something. FUCK YOU ALL!

It angers me when people who've never had a relationship with God tell me how to do it.

MARCH 23, 2000

(MARCH 24, 2000 THURSDAY EVENING 12:45 AM)

I was actually in bed by midnight—but another sleepless night. I've been thinking about the business. I'm going to make a few calls tomorrow—to companies that require my services.

[-]

I am really disgusted by my skinny *and* flabby body. I have (finally) begun to run again. The body needs to get back into shape. I really don't like the way it's looking.

[-]

It occurred to me that the last "steady" girl was Lauren! That was *four* years ago. Almost *half a decade!*

I see people who were single then after a few months, they're hooked up again. What is taking *me* so long? I think there are some serious "look at yourself" assessment needed here—I mean brutal self honesty! (1) I need to shape up. Build a little mass and definition (nothing extreme). (2) I need to improve my dating skills, like *not* having to kiss on the first date, among other things. (3) I need to increase the frequency of the dates that I go on. (4) Perhaps not crucial, but I think it would be helpful to have more hair!

Sergio said that he thought the opportunities for meeting and dating women are everywhere. At that time, I thought he was being just "expressive"—that if we just look, they are there. I'm coming to realize that what he said was not just fluff. I think there *are* lots of women who are looking for this same opportunity that are ready and open.

I think it was myself that was emotionally closed to a lot of this.

APRIL 16, 2000

(10:08 PM, SUNDAY EVENING)

Hey new pen! It should actually be finer than this. Even this is too thick. I'm trying something different for a change. I wanted to be around people this eve. Also, I'm not writing like I normally do, like at 1:00 AM or 6:00 AM. I actually wanted to come down here (Starbucks at 3rd and Wilshire) to hopefully brainstorm for the opera I'm writing with Hank. Right now, I'm more or less a blank. So why not jot down a few of my recent thoughts and events.

The most exciting thing, (which I momentarily thought that I should write in here for fear of "jinxing" it—but then I thought, let's not be superstitious and be grounded in reality) is Tazia. Having met her, it seems that many other women (and men for that matter) seem to operate at a more primitive level. But perhaps I should not write too much more than this because I won't write more than I know. I'm really enjoying her.

[-]

Taxes suck. Tomorrow is the tax deadline. I wish they'd instill a flat tax, like 10%. Everyone pays. Everyone.

[-]

I've been very tired this weekend. Perhaps I'm recovering from my daily workouts. I've been exercising fairly consistently. I think it's starting to show. (I don't like this pen too much).

[-]

Julia's been getting annoying lately. She'll say stuff like, "Okay, I'll call you later today and we'll go out for coffee." Then she never calls. Or "Call me later"…then I'd call and she'll say something like "oh, I have to rearrange my sock drawer…but before that I fell asleep." Once a line is crossed between friends, it's never ever the same. She's really enjoying what this is doing to her ego. But to me it's interesting to see how she reacts when given such a position—a lot like Annie. They're both trying to confirm their identities through external forces. I suppose it's one way to do it. But the resulting perspective is slightly distorted.

I've begun to see that I don't have a lot of respect for many of the girls I've known lately. I'm not comparing them to perfection. But it's little things like courtesy, mannerism, ethics—all very lacking.

I would like to surround myself with more quality people. I never really saw what I've begun to see lately, people in general, women in particular. They are so *unlearned* and primitive.

[illustration-hand written Korean for "useless people"]

쓸 때 없는 사 람

Perhaps I'm being an elitist. Perhaps I'm just beginning to understand myself. What's worse is that they think they're actually much more sophisticated than they really are.

I need to seek and find people—more like artists (true artists), real thinkers, real courtesy and grace, generosity, and so on. Perhaps it will be a lonely search, but I'm already lonely often anyway.

Yes, it is a good goal. I shall find these people and befriend them—

because I think, I hope, we will understand each other better.

That's all for now—still no real idea for the opera. Damn.

APRIL 24, 2000

(10:05 PM, MONDAY EVENING)

Mom and Dad are visiting. I think it was the last time they visited that I realized I get depressed when they're here. Now that I know that that is the reason, I'm dealing with it much better. I remember the last time they were visiting I was really depressed. But as soon as they left, I felt this weight lift off my shoulders and I was quite relieved.

I didn't get a lot of work done today because I was feeling a bit depressed (mom and dad) and a little anxious. But I don't think they're to blame for some of this because I was already beginning to feel like this working by myself. There's this feeling of (I don't want to express it this way, but it was the word that popped into my head) abandonment. It's not a nice feeling—as I am quite familiar with this feeling.

I wondered a little today what it would be like to actually live in France.

[-]

Do I have any "dreams" now? I must, else I wouldn't be so sad sometimes. I think we can express our dreams into goals that aren't necessarily dreams at all, but really a cover up for the fear that one may actually not have one at all.

What is my dream? I'm really, really not sure. There's almost this *voice* that says that one must have a dream, or wonderful goal to work toward. Again, it's a voice that calls for a dream—rather than a dream that calls for me. They're like voices from the devil…put into my head…as if to say that we *need* more. But really, I don't really want or need much. I'm enjoying the things I have, and beyond that, it's all 'icing' on the cake.

If anything, I think I would still like to try a few things I haven't tried. More traveling! Yes! I love going places. It would be really cool to have a traveling partner, for sure.

MAY 30, 2000

(10:15 PM, TUESDAY)

I'm at Santa Monica Pier to jot down a few notes on the 'fork' ahead. I sense that I shall be moving out of the country for further exploration and living. At first, I wanted to make sure I'm not running away from any responsibility or duty to others such as friends and family.

The thing is, I think they'd be excited for me. I'm guessing somewhere around September or October. There's the money situation to resolve as well. It seems a little complicated but hopefully it is not too bad.

(These benches at the pier are not very comfy).

I'm trying to understand if my next move is one for "settlement" or for the sake of having an adventure. I wonder perhaps that I should live in a couple more places or even move before deciding to "settle down." I hate that word because it implies so many institutional gestures. But really, for me, settling down means that your heart, mind, and body have come to an agreement about a certain place.

I think the reason I returned to L.A. was because this city (for me) isn't already a certain place. It was still generic enough. But how things have changed here in the 10-15 years since I left. It was a holding place.

Now I must decide because I shouldn't stay too long in the transition.

I am now thinking of two places: Paris and Auckland, New Zealand. I was going to make a list of reasons to stay and reasons to move. But the fact is, I've chosen in my heart, already, to move. I think it's a matter of where, when, and how.

I shall start some lists nonetheless.

THINGS TO DO BEFORE I LEAVE:

- Grand Canyon
- Yellowstone

THE POSITIVES TO MOVING TO PARIS:

- Beautiful

- Appreciate the Arts
- Learn new language
- New Friends
- See more of Europe
- Idea sounds cool/magical factor
- I may be more appreciated for my perspective
- More open minded
- I'm more akin to their view of life compared to U.S. and even to Korea

THE POSITVES OF STAYING IN L.A.:

- Career
- Family
- Friends
- Lots to do
- Don't have to do anything

THE POSITIVES OF MOVING TO AUCKLAND:

- New friends
- Transition (Language easy)
- Sailing
- Beautiful
- Serene and Peaceful
- Friendly
- Need good designers
- Water everywhere

THE NEGATIVES OF MOVING TO PARIS:

- Difficult Transition
- Possible rude French People
- Possible isolation
- Andy there ("reporter")

THE NEGATIVES OF MOVING TO AUCKLAND

- Possibly bored and/or restless
- Possible Island Fever
- "Foreigner" factor

THE NEGATIVES OF STAYING IN L.A.:

- Traffic
- Ignorant unappreciative people
- Career
- No Romance! (I don't think it's just bad luck…I'm not appreciated here)

OBSTACLES

- Money
- Language
- Job

I know that the firs thing I really have to do is make a decision. Then everything else will come more naturally. If I thought that I'd be seriously considering moving to France so soon, I don't know that I'd have started the business. Buy you can't always see what's beyond the horizon until you make a move of some sort, even when it seems ridiculous or out of place.

JUNE 9, 2000

(JUNE 10, 2000 FRIDAY NIGHT 12:18 AM)

Two weeks before my trip to New Zealand. I've had much on my mind these past few weeks—everything from moving to New Zealand or France to what I should do to meet someone. I'm just really, really tired. I've also had been thinking about what Daron had said the other night at the birthday dinner when Zarah cancelled out on dinner: half jokingly, he said something like, "Well you know how Insung's friends are all very flakey." Something snapped inside and a tremendous sadness came over me. I was sad of course because it was true. And I was also sad because it was himself that had flaked out in the first place on my real birthday—the irony! He decided to throw a birthday dinner then chickened out because it would take too much effort and resources on his end. I was really embarrassed for myself…as if I was *making* him do this thing for me—because none of my friends would actually do that for me. I am *really* embarrassed that that's how he thinks of me. After all these years, my friendship means that much, that little.

Perhaps I just need time away. But incidences like these are quite disheartening.

I begun to realize how important airports mean to friendships. In my estimation it is those you trust or are friends with that you are willing to take someone to the airport. Not only was I appalled when he told me to take the shuttle to the airport, I started to wake up to his state of mind and heart—even more appalled that he had the nerve to ask me to take *him* to the airport, which I did anyway.

But what was most revealing of all, when he said that my friends were flakey, it subtly implied, without intention that he was really *not* my friend.

I cannot believe what I am writing. I mean, how can anyone say what I'm saying after all these years of friendship? It doesn't seem to make any sense.

But it's exactly like the story, "Flowers for Algernon." Charlie thought his co-workers at the bakery were his friends when all along they were just laughing at him; a butt of their jokes. I am showing signs of waking up and this is what I see—a bunch of people laughing at me. They're all laughing at me because they have nothing better to do with their lives.

JUNE 11, 2000

(JUNE 12, 2000 SUNDAY NIGHT/MONDAY MORNING 12:03 AM)

I wanted some time to pass to write again about Daron and my other friends. I wanted to make sure I was not in some sort of emotional ball when I wrote some of the things that I did write.

I think the issue isn't so much about Daron or anyone else but about my need on self-reliance. I think that I think of friends as people you rely on and trust and so forth. But other people seem to think of friends as people you do stuff with.

I've been thinking a lot about friendship and what it means to me. We don't always agree on what that is.

In some ways I'm glad I wasn't born super rich, super handsome, or something like that. Perhaps because I wouldn't have known who would've wanted to be friends because they liked me, or because I would have made them feel important.

The latter is a very important point. This is because I too have realized more or less recently that I sometimes wanted to go out with certain girls because it would have made me feel important, at least to myself.

I am hoping that I can be honest enough with myself to cut out the bull. It seems much of the "keeping up of appearances" is done through some sort of a need for approval. I cannot condemn myself totally for doing this. After all, I am human. But so much of it is to be accepted by society, culture, friends, and family.

When I truly and honestly, as best I could, think about what I need and want, I don't think I need or want all that much. I would like to be reasonably comfortable. But overall, I think I'd like to go through the rest of this life by "traveling light."

JUNE 14, 2000

(11:46 PM, WEDNESDAY NIGHT)

Two days before I leave for New Zealand. I don't want to live alone anymore. Perhaps that is the fork I have reached in the road. Finding the right person seems like an impossible task. People tell me that I'm too picky. In some ways, I suppose I am. But I see that many women don't seem like a good match for me.

Sometimes I think someone might be right but once I get to know her a little, we have little in common. Else, the other party loses interest or finds fault in myself. I don't know what I'd do without this journal. It's like having a therapist or friend except that you get to keep the recoding of the events and conversations that took place.

AUGUST 13, 2000

(11:52 PM, SUNDAY EVENING)

Just came back from Tracy's dinner party. She and her other belly-dancing friends did a little performance.

What a crazy weekend. It was Adam's 40th birthday and there was a dinner party on Friday at Luna Park; a dinner at the Ranch House in Ojai.

I've been a little embarrassed over the weekend. Renée tried to (more or less) set me up with Linda. She (Linda) stayed over (crashed) at my place Friday night and then at Rick's Sunday night. I had asked Linda out on a date only to get a very hesitant "it doesn't mean we won't go out in the future." I said, "you can so no." She's actually a very nice girl. But perhaps because I was being set up (because I was being watched) I didn't feel all that relaxed. And in some ways, I thought we weren't quite a good match. But I think a part of me asked her out because I felt Renée worked so hard to do something nice for me. Part of it was because I did find her attractive. And part of it was because, although I wasn't wow'd by her, I thought I should proceed because of her good qualities (such as manners and so forth). But such things are a two way street.

[-]

Also at the dinner table in Ojai, there was talk of religion and how one would raise a child when the two parents come from 2 different religions. That conversation had made me sad. I didn't contribute much to the conversation. I was too busy wondering where God was in my life. That had made me sad, I think most of all.

When I was much younger, I used to have much conversation with God—like he was always there watching over me. It wasn't until I became a Christian that the feeling of the presence of God, had left. I know it says in the Bible that no one goes to the Father without passing through the Son. Yet, I don't know the son at all. It's not that I didn't want to (because that would make so many things fit so neatly)…but I couldn't or wouldn't.

It has also been written that the power of the word of the Lord is written in the *hearts* of men. Such things as the beatitudes are there in the heart, but the doctrine doesn't fit in. and anytime I have to prey to Jesus, I feel like I'm blocking the passage way to God.

Yet, I miss God. I miss singing to him.

AUGUST 14, 2000

(7:34 AM, MONDAY MORNING)

I thought it would be important to record my thoughts and feelings this morning.

I was waking up with that feeling of 'uneasiness' again just like some pages back. But this time, I see the direct connection to the rejection. It's the feeling you get from the result of a heartbreak, or large emotional grief. These feelings of abandonment are not pleasant at all. I think somewhere deep inside, I'm beginning to believe that perhaps I will remain unmarried. I mean, for so long, in the back of your mind, you always know that someday, you will get married. But now the possibilities are there. And it's a strange thought—a strange reality.

[-]

I am now preparing myself for the possibility of moving to France. I have been scared, quite scared. The most frightening thing is not the language or cultural barriers. In fact, I see that as a welcoming challenge. But the biggest fear is that of regret. Seeing the fork in the road ahead, it is difficult and…no, impossible, to predict. Which is the road that I'll have the least amount of regrets?

I know in some ways that my "body" is getting heavier, meaning that my age is perhaps catching up to me. It's amazing to see the depth of human tenacity, courage, and strength when situations call for them. Right now, I feel I have one final hold before falling off the end of the rope. Or perhaps another way to look at it is, I have one more reach from hanging on the edge of the cliff before pulling myself up to safety.

"If you see a fork in the road, take it." –Yogi Berra

It's a funny thing, forks in the road that is. You can probably not see one for a decade or you may see one every couple of months. And the thing about some forks in the road is that many times you can foresee them in the distance. But it isn't til some situation puts you face to face with that decision that you actually deal with them.

My France fork keeps coming back. I don't know why at all. It's a strange little obsession. And the fork is very close. It's almost as if I have already chosen which path to take. I seem to be controlling my environment to put myself in that situation.

When Linda said no, my very, very first thoughts were that of moving to France, as if she was some sort of the last signpost.

My last fork in the road was NYU to L.A. Somehow the journey stopped (or seemed to) since I moved to L.A. It will have ben 5 years this January.

And honestly, I am not really living my true life. What I am about to do (moving) seems to be a test of faith—to build courage—for no real reason other than to connect myself on a deeper level with myself and with God. How crazy does that sound?

AUGUST 14, 2000

(11:53 PM, MONDAY EVENING)

Maturity is a strange word that I don't quite understand. Many people judge maturity by the "responsibilities" one takes on, such as holding a steady job or caring for your family. Another way to look at it, which is closer to the way I think about it, is that of walking your talking—meaning that different people are "different" indeed and while many (perhaps most) have similar ideas of this maturity, I almost see it as the opposite way—to cast off so-called "responsibilities" and go into a blind walk. (I'm tired. I hope I'm explaining that right).

Maturity is like the word "good." To say that something is good is to say that something functions in the way it was designed. For example, a good chair is one that holds a person comfortably and with strength to keep him safe. Similarly, a person who is coming into maturity is one that is filling in the form of the designed soul or person. I think people must have different forms of maturity. Else, there would be no artists, philosophers, priests, or to some degree, scientists. Everyone would have 2 kids and a steady job. It seems that what stands between a person and his potential maturity is that of time and faculty. It takes some time to develop the necessary skills to handle the position of self-control. And without the necessary faculties, be it sunshine and water, or parental love or born-strength or wit, it would also be difficult if not impossible to do what is called for, from within.

Oftentimes, I see the vision of what I ought or could be. I then realize that the faculties to get there are often missing or undeveloped. Those times, I get discouraged.

OCTOBER 11, 2000

(11:46 PM, WEDNESDAY)

A brief moment to write down my thoughts. A few things that are going on: (1) Business seems to be doing okay. I am working on a Guinness Bus Shelter. (2) I've been contemplating the purchase of a motorcycle.

On the latter note, I was caught between two models. One is the Indian Scout, priced at around $20,000. The other is a Harley-Davidson Sportster priced at around $7,000. I really like both bikes for different reasons. At one instance, I equated the Scout as, realizing that I've become (and becoming even more so) the person I was meant to be. And I equated the Sportster as a little boy lost and playing with his toys. But at another instance, I equated the Sportster as a motorcycle with little affectations while the Scout was too polished.

I'm not sure where I'll travel to next. But the purchase of a motorcycle may play a part on whether I travel at all in the near to mid future.

A few other objects in the works: (1) Haunted House Video (2) Music Videos for Ave Maria.

OCTOBER 28, 2000

(7:08 AM, SATURDAY)

Interesting dream. I know I remember only parts. But I think they're significant enough to note. First part, I was in a small plane (like a Cessna). I was sitting in front next to the pilot. I don't think the pilot was my father, even though after I awoke, I sensed it was someone like that. But I don't think it was him. Anyway we were in trouble (the plane). We had to land. Luckily we barely landed, but safely. Some mechanic or airport worker tells me that we can still land but not amphibiously. The airport was a fairly small airport, smaller than Burbank.

Next segment: sort of vague.

There were these people, almost like hunting tribesmen who are slipping down this muddy hill. At the bottom of the hill was a giant spear. They all got speared and killed. In my mind I was responsible, or partly responsible for doing so.

[illustration-spear death]

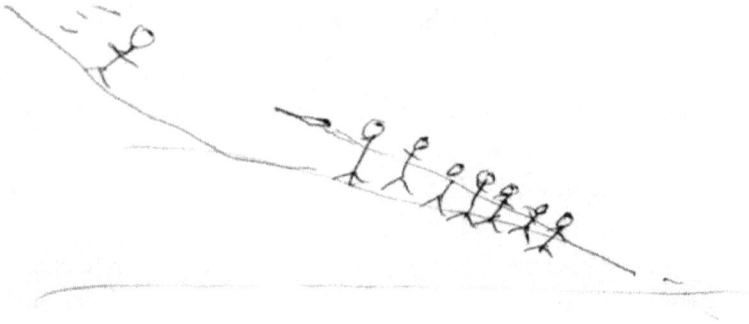

Another segment: I'm in this large house or mansion or something roomy like that. And in the walls were these "things", these men again (or tribesmen or whatever) being chased out of the walls, like they were being flushed out. Then something or someone important got killed. I think I killed him. I left this house. There was no exterior as I recall. I'm not sure where I went. But when I returned after a brief moment, the house had completely transformed. I think it was now a hotel. And the new management had remodeled the entire suite. Everything was that green marble. The floor, wall, ceiling, bathtub, everything was in green marble. I think I vaguely remember a chandelier in there. It was to the point where it was done in poor taste. But I realized it was covered over like this to hide a terrible death that happened not long ago. I remember just now, the stairwell going up to the main door were worn and broken. There were pieces of wood and splintering. I started getting an eerie feeling as I was standing there looking around at all this green marble. I looked over at the dining room and there were these four young women dressed in those old European dresses with those strange accordion pleated neck rings (collars), playing cards. I understood their event as some sort of church function. I decided to leave this place. As I walked out I was in this sort of large hallway with windows on one side. There were lots of people standing around and chatting. As I was leaving this place, near the front door, I saw this girl who looked like, Yvonne Feinstein. She didn't seem to recognize me since it had been so long since high school. So, I yelled out "Yvonne!" She turned around. She smiled as she looked at me. She said or thought "Oh, my God." She looked beautiful and exactly as I remembered her, still with that same hair style. She told me she had been married for 2 years. I met her husband. He was there also. Not particularly hand-some (or ugly), but perhaps a little overbearing. I told him he married a great girl. He muttered something that I can't remember. That was that. (The end).

As I recall now, it's possible that girl's spirit could have been Lauren. I mean, that it "felt" like her. Visually, she was still Yvonne.

DECEMBER 5, 2000

(12:47 AM, TUESDAY 'MORNING')

There is only one thing that is more expensive than the cost of free-dom, and that is the cost of love. While freedom is the love of self, love is giving freedom to the other.

Yet it does not seem logical that we cannot share or give something that does not belong to us either in heart or by understanding.

Question is, shouldn't we already have it before we can give it?

For many people, it would seem, it has ben instilled in them at youth's age by loving parents. But what of those that weren't so fortu-nate? What of them? If not by the Grace of life or God, how would it be possible for many of these children and adult-children to obtain or understand this gift or hope? How would it be possible for them to experience this part of life that would seem so pertinent to existence?

DECEMBER 6, 2000

(12:06 AM, WEDNESDAY "MORNING")

[nothing written]

DECEMBER 18, 2000

(2:32 AM, MONDAY MORNING)

Couldn't sleep at all. I accidentally fell asleep in the afternoon for three hours. I can't believe New Year's is upon us once again. I called Stacy this evening. She seems to be doing quite well. (I'm tired but can't sleep…it's awful). I will be heading for Vegas once again. I think it will be nice. I've been feeling the urge lately to exercise or start doing some sports again. The body is craving it—and it kind of needs it too.

2001 Dogma

FEBRUARY 15, 2001

(11:03 PM, THURSDAY EVENING)

It's a good time to write. I haven't done so in awhile. I'm pretty clear-headed and pretty well balanced. There are a few thoughts on my mind. Lots going on. Film school prep. Dating. Coming to terms with my age. Moving my office.

There are a lot of things floating around in my head. Will I get into a film school? If so, will I go to film school? I know it's a very important time. But it's so difficult to know. As far as film school, it seems my main concern is, would I be more successful going to film school than doing it on my own? Honestly, I don't think I will be any more or less creative in the work I produce. But if I really want to succeed as a filmmaker, I should let go and go for it!

If I am a graphic designer that makes films on the side then I will always be a graphic designer (that makes films on the side). If my reason to continue what I do now, i.e. design for money and film on the side, is to hold onto what little security or "relative" success, then I shall have failed in my life. It's difficult to say whether my reasons (to continue as I am) are those of satisfactory acceptance and contentment of what I have, or if it is a way for me to bow out of a future situation that consists of much (more) hard work and questionable financial situations.

And I can't just choose the latter merely because it sounds more noble. Of course, the questionable financial situation will also be a hindrance to my social and romantic life. That's another reason continuing as I am sounds attractive.

When it comes down to it, it's a matter of what I believe and how much faith I have in it. Faith—the measure of my conviction. Action—the measure of my courage. But if deep down inside I believe that I can't make it as a filmmaker, wouldn't it be wise to know and consider my limitations?

Nobody can tell me how to make this decision because in the end, it is myself I have to face—to know that I lived *my* life, my way, and that I can look at myself in the end and know that I have little or no regrets.

It's not what I have to do in life that makes this decision difficult, but rather what I *believe* I have to do. Really, I don't know that anyone needs to do anything or be anyone. Yet, somehow, if I don't do it, it seems like I'm cheating myself.

I think I have many irrational fears regarding important decisions. Regardless, I have them. For example, I think that I will be all alone if I take the road to film school. It's the same fear I had when I wanted to design yachts.

But perhaps the truth is, I will be with me—the most important person. Perhaps I've been afraid to be alone, with *me*, to face me, understand me, and to be in conflict. Yet it is something to be worked *through* not around.

I am not physically alone, but psychologically and spiritually, I am. I think for many people it may be natural and perhaps when we were children.

I think that's the most important thing in my life right now is to go through this portal alone, to be with…me. Then emerge on the other side, in my own skin. Perhaps I was avoiding this for quite some time. It seems this journey through the portal is a necessary step.

It's hard to know. And perhaps I won't even know that it happened. But those are the steps that appear below me.

FEBRUARY 27, 2001

(9:30 PM, TUESDAY)

Daron blew me off for the Saturday opening.

MARCH 28, 2001

(2:27 AM, WEDNESDAY)

Couldn't sleep. Took a little nap in the afternoon. I wish I wasn't struggling so much with money, love and artistic goals.

JULY 11, 2001

A few notes: I've been with Christine for about 2 months now. Things seem to going fairly well. My heart seems a little anxious this evening. Actually, it's been that way the last few days. I felt my heart grieving about something. I wasn't sure what exactly. I know Christine's dad died a week and a half ago.

Something seems to be draining my heart. I'm not sure what it is. At first I thought possibly that her dad's death had something to do with it. But I don't think so.

I thought possibly that at Linda Hoier's party, something was triggered when Christine was rubbing tattoos on this guy's arm. It was very strange.

I didn't understand why a girl goes to a party with her boyfriend starts shamelessly flirting with other guys. Then when I tried to enquire, she pulled out a tattoo and said, "here, you go play with them" —pointing to some girls. Very, very strange.

This tells me one of two things. One, she does that to make me jealous for control reasons. Or two, she does that because I'm not really what she wants, but is too scared to go after what she does want.

The worse comment was when the guy got up to get another drink, she turns to me (and Daron and Mark) and says "he's too weird anyway."

"Too weird?" What was she qualifying this guy for? And the "anyway" inferring that the consolation was still a safer choice?

It wasn't even the fact that she was flirting, which itself can be bad or good. But understanding her mindset was a bit frightening. It was as if there were no "regulators" for her behaviors. Almost seemed that she had no concept of consequences or a sense of the physical reality.

Very, very disturbing.

The first time I witnessed something like this was when she walked in my door. We were just starting to go out and we hadn't physically seen each other for a little while. She walked in. She dropped her jacket to the floor directly off her shoulders and walked into my living room…as if there was no jacket, no floor, no closet, or even a concept of one. It was as if she was dreaming and she took the jacket off in her dream. And in her dream the jacket simply vanished. I saw for a brief moment, a glimpse on what she saw. But I also saw the jacket fall to the floor landing somewhere between the vinyl tile entry way and the carpet. It would have seemed okay if she threw it somewhere: in the corner, on the couch, or even in my face—anywhere but out of her mind.

She seems to be living mostly in her mind, er, her mind's idea of the world. And while everyone really interprets the world through their minds as well, there is an acknowledgement by others of the common reality. It seems much of her reality is fabricated. This was actually one of my first gripes with her. I didn't feel that she was involved with me, but rather someone she fabricated in her mind, someone much greater than I would admit to being—a case, perhaps, of self-deception covered over by either fear or pain or both.

What's frightening is that I see in her, what I can now see in my past. To realize I had similar traits is a little disturbing.

And much of the pain suffered was really the realization that my ideas of reality were untrue, disrupting my elaborate systems of justification and validations. The pain suffered were less of the heart, and really more of the mind and knowing the shame of who I was—or wasn't.

And my inability to commit to some "one" thing was the inability to identify myself—for the fear that the self discovery will happen during the course of this one thing and that perhaps I would be in the wrong place, at the right time. That was it.

I got it.

JULY 12, 2001

(1:23 AM, THURSDAY EVENING)

(4:07 AM)

I've actually been up all this time. Actually just in bed, not asleep.

The more I think about Christine, the more I realize that it's not the right direction. Perhaps it is severe to call it this, but the term "Hitler-itis" comes to mind. And the term "The road to hell is paved with good intentions."

She seems to have this need to control everything—and "I want a happy world" seems like some strange, albeit innocently packaged way of saying that there is something terribly wrong in the state of Denmark.

She is planning *way* too much. No, I mean *way, way* too much. And I'm one of those pieces in her mind, not a person. Very strange and disturbing. Yet I know what she's thinking. It's almost as if she's out of control and seems like she's seeking discipline or defined boundaries from me.

OCTOBER 7, 2001

(12:49 AM, SUNDAY "MORNING"/SATURDAY EVENING)

There are so many lonely people. It's frightening. Everything seems to be hidden within the façades of happiness, wealth, health, or whatever.

Every face has a story.

I have been thinking a lot about faith lately. Faith is difficult to come by. It seems we really don't exercise it 'til we run out of options—until reality doesn't make sense any more. I came back from this girl's party tonight in Manhattan Beach. It was filled mainly with young good-looking people that seemed kind of clueless and rather dull. I'm sure it was their lack of experience in the world.

I'm not sure what I wanted to say. I'm tired. It's getting late.

School has generally been a fairly good experience so far. It's something I'd promised myself. So even 'though I will be around 38 and penniless by the time I graduate, it seems I do in fact need that validation.

I hate being poor. But when I had a job that paid well, it was quite depressing to think that "that" was it.

I think people have certain things that they need to do or achieve in life to be able to say "I *lived* my life." I think for myself, one is that graduate degree and the other is to have a long meaningful relationship. Children may be another one, but as of now, that seems kind of distant.

Why is love *so* difficult? It seems to require the most out of a person. It demands so much energy and honesty. I don't see how any couple can make it. I just can't believe it's that complicated.

I wish I could pray for more faith. But I know that that's impossible since the definition itself require that we take the *initiative* to believe, the *energy* to believe, the *will* to believe.

That requires courage.

I just wish and hope, and pray then for courage. Everything requires a choice and initiative.

(9:25 AM)

Consciousness feels like a curse with no relief in sight. Consciousness=alone. It's as if I'm one of very few people who seem to be awake. So many people are robots completely unaware.

I wrote back a little while ago that when I go to sleep, my heart speaks in that domain; when I'm awake, my mind seems to take over. (Not sure what I was going to say).

Sunday mornings are so wonderful. I don't have to be anywhere. It's just so peaceful. I wish everyday was like Sunday.

NOVEMBER 12, 2001

(1:09 AM, MONDAY EVENING)

I just ate some rice and kimchee. It's been raining outside. So, it's a little colder. I usually have nightmares if I go to bed hungry and I sleep cold.

I've been up so I thought I'd write a little.

I've come a long way I think. Emotionally, I find myself in better control. And in some ways, it makes me quite happy that I can do that.

FAITH is such an important thing in life. It's difficult to emphasize how monumentally significant it is, to living everyday.

I've been living alone for a while. And I think on the whole, it's been very good to me—at least in terms of my growth. But I want to live in a house and be a family member again. I'm not sure that means having a child of my own or perhaps just a wife, but it is a strong desire and need.

I think religion was invented so that we can exercise our faith—because faith is too abstract and without form. By having a deity in some contextual form, it is easier for our minds to understand what our spirit seeks.

Most children have this innate faith. When we're older, we seem to lose it. Else, it becomes a constant choice to believe.

I only say this because I'm beginning to believe again—though not as a child but as an adult.

I'm beginning to see the inklings of this choice for my life. It feels really good. And I feel gratitude somehow to someone or something.

NOVEMBER 13, 2001

(11:16 PM, TUESDAY EVENING)

"Disillusion comes only to the illusioned. One cannot be disillusioned of what one never puts faith in." —Dorothy Thompson

"The attainment of an ideal is often the beginning of a disillusion."—Stanley Baldwin

"The longer you stay in one place, the greater your chances of disillusionment." —Art Spander

"We can be of little service to our fellows until we become disillusioned without being embittered."—Lord Darling

Disillusion: Noun: Freeing from false belief or illusion (dictionary.com)

NOVEMBER 15, 2001

(9:21 AM, THURSDAY MORNING)

The words are, "paranoid, neurotic, and faithless" as I have read some past entries from a few years' past. In fact I think it goes in that order—perhaps naiveté should precede "paranoid." Again, I quote William S. Burroughs "Paranoia is getting your facts straight." And again, I have woken up with feelings of fear today. It happens when I'm disillusioned or disheartened, when I have put faith in something.

Naiveté: We wish to break out of this cave. We hear sounds from the outside.

Paranoia: We break out of the cave and find it frightening (we get the facts straight)

Neurotic: Happens when we can't decide what to do about it.

Faithless: Happens when the small attempts did not work and lack courage to try again.

Cynical: When we give up and believe that things cannot be changed.

Faith: Obtained by exercising courage and also the beginning of the civilized person.

Of course, we should put our faith in something unchangeable. When my faith in God was destroyed, I'd become quite affected like above. But perhaps it was my concept of God that got destroyed, the dogma.

It's a very strange concept. My new "God" is much more abstract, much bigger. It's something I have no control over, yet it's something I believe in. or to put it another way, I sense that everything's going to be alright. I don't have to protect "God." It would almost be silly of me to go and search for a book on religion or theology because I don't think any of it would be necessary or capable of explaining how I relate in my faith—though I'm sure it would be interesting reading.

[illustration-timeline]

Timeline : not precise

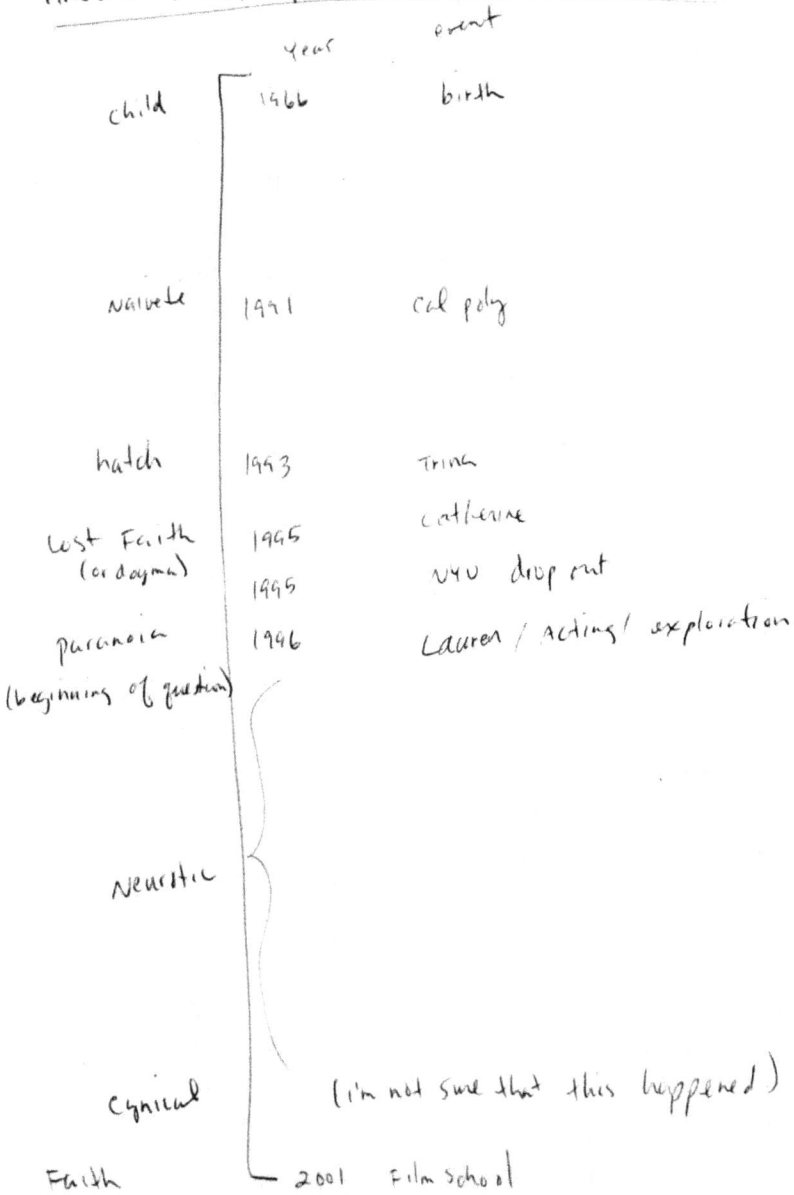

	year	event
child	1966	birth
Naïveté	1991	Cal poly
hatch	1993	Trinh
Lost Faith (or dogma)	1995	catherine
	1995	UYU drop out
paranoia (beginnings of question)	1996	Lauren / Acting / exploration
Neurotic		
Cynical		(I'm not sure that this happened)
Faith	2001	Film school

NOVEMBER 23, 2001

(12:21 AM, THRUSDAY EVENING, THANKSGIVING)

I ate so much. I'm quit sleepy, but I thought I'd write a few words. I actually don't feel like sharing some things in here. I kind of want to keep it to myself—as if this journal is not a part of me.

Actually, it's as though I want to handle it internally. I want to deal with it. So my feelings I won't share. But I would like to note a few events.

I just shot the second half of "The Box." It went quite well. I will have to edit this weekend. I will also paint "Felix The Cat" laughing—with his bag of tricks.

I made my first pumpkin pie today. It was a hit. Mark came down from Oregon to see Daron. I got a call from Harry wishing me a Happy Thanksgiving. I would like to read Anne Karenina over Christmas.

I'm very tired.

NOVEMBER 25, 2001

(11:27 AM, SUNDAY MORNING)

Just got out of bed (still in bed actually). An important thought came over me this morning. How do I explain this? It part, it comes from having faith, in believing in one's self and situation. To recall, before I was going out with Lauren, I remember how determined I was and how much I *believed* that I could have her be with me. And it came true. The difference then was that I didn't have as much sense as I do now, which made it difficult to go beyond what I have imagined. In other words, I hadn't imagined, or truly believed beyond my fears that I would really be with her beyond the "getting" stage. I "got" her, but I didn't keep her because I didn't *plan* or *think* beyond that breakthrough stage. It was as though my main focus was to "break through." And when I broke through, I didn't know what to do because my plan of attack was only for the "breakthrough" period. I think I'm repeating myself now.

When I think about my relative graphic design success, I *know* that I could have gotten much, much further in terms of both monetary success and affluence. But the problem was that my heart wasn't completely into it. I didn't want to "succeed" in being something I *wasn't*. Perhaps it's like saying I didn't want to succeed as a garbage man—though the comparison may be a little extreme. It is in a way childish; a little perfectionistic. But that is what I understand.

Now to my point: it is when I truly believe, that I take *action*. And when I take action, it tends to come true—like the self-fulfilling prophecy. If I were to now prophesize what I woke up believing I will tell you the two things that came into me this morning. I believe success in two areas: One is in a filmmaking career—a brilliant one. The other is in finding and keeping a happy and wonderful marriage and wife.

I love Angie. I love her dearly.

I love being with her; spending time with her. she's the person's equivalent of the Ocean. I don't have to be anywhere else, and time passes as one, no future or past—only the infinite present. I'm so attracted to her yet she is like my little sister. I want to protect her and take care of her. And my happiness seems to flow from my heart. Making her laugh bring me so much joy. I am not afraid to love her.

DECEMBER 7, 2001

(5:23 AM, FRIDAY)

It's the end of the semester with only the finals week left. A few words of concern: (1) Money. I need money badly. I'm not sure how next semester will work. I may sell the car. That would help a lot. I will also cut off any extraneous expenses. I need to finish school. I need some financial advice.

I really need to grow up. I'm a little frightened also because I'm 35 and still in school; I make the same bad decisions in love affairs; I don't have money. How about a little faith *now?* It's quite frightening. Some people think I'm brave, but they don't see how scared I could be. I'm not rich right now, and it's difficult to let go of some things like the car. It's incredibly hard to go back to a certain lifestyle when you're used to certain luxuries.

Will my values change as I get older? Why do I live such an isolated life? I realize I'm sacrificing some quality of life by taking the road I have with filmmaking. I just need to keep everything in perspective.

Don't be too frightened. I wish I could get a girl like Angie but my "dowry" isn't big enough. As sad as that is, that's the truth. I'm poor. No smart girl will go for a poor guy. And no smart, beautiful girl will *ever* go for a poor guy.

I know I'm perhaps a little superstitious, but the non-believers seem to be at church picking out husbands. It's quite messed up.

I think Daron and I work well together because he's so grounded and I offer a little (or a lot) of "what if's."

Social class, education, and perhaps religion seem to be large factors in determining a working relationship between married people. A girl doesn't want a promise. A girl wants a wealthy prince.

I'd like to think that I'd build a relationship on principles and I know that that is probably the value of the working class—but money seems to rule everything else. The value of money is a very, very hard lesson.

Some things:

-Sell car

-Get roommate

-Cut other expenses

-Freelance onsite

Socioeconomics is a very, very hard lesson. I'm quite low on the totem pole: No cash, no status, aging body, third racial status. It sucks.

2002 Respect for Women

SEPTEMBER 13, 2002

(SEPTEMBER 14, 2002, 12:50 AM)

I don't write as often as I used to. In some ways, it's good. It means I don't *need* to. In some ways, if I write things down I don't deal with them internally. Sometimes it is very important that I do write some things.

Tonight is not one of them.

Tomorrow: Crew Drill. Choreography. Bald Cap.

All I say is to walk in faith.

NOVEMBER 3, 2002

I'm eating my lunch today, a tuna fish sandwich. And I realize something important. I realize I had very little respect for women. The realization sort of dawned on me over the last few days. One, I was thinking about Breanna and her constant struggle to make this documentary on Croatia. I think it's really difficult to be a woman filmmaker, especially if you are attractive. I questioned my motives about my involvement with her project. I thought: Would I be so willing to cross the Atlantic with my own money to make (or help make) someone else's film, especially if this someone else was a man? I thought *perhaps*—because it really can be an amazing experience. But honestly, I couldn't answer that fairly. Then I actually thought about what she had to do amongst getting "unnecessary" attention from the male helpers. Then I was sad for her. She is making a film she feels so compelled to make because it is so close to her. Yet sometimes all I could think about is whether she might be a good mate. I'm of course allowed to imagine. But sometimes it wasn't appropriate. The point is, not everyone (not every female) is like my mother. I'm not doomed to the kind of love that I learned from her. Her intentions were certainly good and I have benefited in many ways. But not every woman is to be totally controlled or be controlled by them. This is indeed important in understanding my patterns of failure with relationships—in order to succeed.

It appeared that once a woman "submitted" emotionally to me, I tended to treat her with disrespect, as if I had total control, power and authority. When in fact, when someone *trusted* enough to be vulnerable, I sometimes did not see that it was really a gift, not a sign of weakness.

I really, truly hope that I can respect women for more than just objects of desire or a breeder of our race. I'm glad, perhaps feeling lucky, to know this—and to have them around. I am enough. Sometimes I value women so that they'd be a worthwhile pursuit, escalating them sometimes to unreasonable places of expectations. Sometimes I degrade them if I am not attracted to them (the opposite) in order to not have a relationship with them. I certainly don't think I'm unique in this behavior. Nor am I here punishing myself in shame. But it is good to note this, so that I may move on in hopes for a fulfilling, intimate relationship with a woman.

2003 Living in the Now

JANUARY 14, 2003

(8:07 AM, TUESDAY MORNING, AT DESK)

I thought this is important enough to write down. Of the much prog-ress I'd been making on improving myself, one of the large elements that hindered me, not only from relationships, but perhaps in other areas as well is that...when, in the past, I started going out on dates, in the initial stages, I would get all nervous. And in this period, my body and mind would interpret it as something *wrong*—and perhaps it's not so abnormal since it is a foreign element that I was not used to. And in doing so, I sent out signals and probably words as well that said there *really was* something wrong.

When in fact, it is something *so* right. And I should treat it like so. I should be happy and express what it truly is—a gift perhaps, an opportunity to make things grow, a chance to nurture and a chance to allow myself the trust to be nurtured.

JANUARY 17, 2003

(10:00 PM, FRIDAY EVENING)

I was in the process of starting the rewrite of the Casper Jones story. I became frustrated. It's a mess. It was written in a hurry to get it done within the given amount of time in England. As I was about to do the rewrite I realize the rewrite will likely not fare better. Also, I am not generally happy with the script. This finally brings me to my point. I am not happy, not because it's a bad script, but because it's just not original or that interesting. I've been learning film at Chapman nearing two years now. I am quite appreciative of the basics and grounding in storytelling. But now I'd like to turn my (unhurried) energy into creat-ing a beautiful cinematic experience. I want the medium itself to play a role in the telling (not just the story) but in the sensuality of it all. I am very, very interested in how music and sound play alongside visuals that go beyond the three-point lighting or talking heads. A rave is to a party—is what my vision is to film.

I need to allow myself enough money and especially time to create something I could truly be proud of—or at least feel it's an honest expression. All the other shit is boring.

As I'm thinking—perhaps for the next and final semester of classes I'd like to experiment heavily with the visuals and sound system—to incorporate those elements into the storytelling. No, I mean *Experience Telling*.

NOVEMBER 28, 2003

(2:32 AM, FRIDAY NIGHT/SATURDAY MORNING)

Came back from seeing "The Missing" with a Hungarian girl I met on the Promenade. Decent movie. She disappeared after the movie. (It kind of made me amused). I was in bed but thought it was important enough to get up and write.

There is a slow and genuine confidence building in me—the kind that comes from relying on facts and knowledge, rather than perception from ego.

The thing I've been thinking a lot about lately is how I'm much better coping with the external world. When I deal in reality, to be fully aware of the here and now, to strive to understand the underpinnings of some strange behavior, event, or circumstances, I am *so relieved* to know that everything is going to be okay. This sounds simple enough, like child's play, but to put it into practice is so incredibly liberating. There is a sense of well being, that everything is all right in the world.

This is *quite* a revelation considering how difficult, or near impossible it was to get past that fear and perception. I believe I'm *finally, finally* entering the adult brain. It is such an amazing feeling.

2004 Filmmaking Hell

[Thesis Year—did not write]

2005 Longing for the Southwest

FEBRUARY 14, 2005

(2:07 AM, MONDAY MORNING)

It's interesting that I frequently write at 2:00 in the morning. Film school is finished. I've come to another crossroads. I've been agonizing over a decision lately—stay in L.A. or move to Portland.

I am writing because I've come to the conclusion that I don't want to do either.

Here are some thoughts: Dirt, Southern Hemisphere, Some body of water, Not a big city, Small fishing village type of place, writing.

I believe it's a spiritual longing of some sort. Of course two big concerns come to mind: (1) How do I make a living and pay off my debts? (2) Will I have to learn a new language?

AUGUST 31, 2005

(MORNING)

A Dream the night of August 30, 2005

A beautiful naked woman who was delighted to go into the water (warm?) and purposely drown herself.

[illustration-red plastic tub woman]

red plastic tub

-Red plastic tub

-I picture a red dress she had on

-Replaced my old couch to a different part of the room (TV room?)

-Got a new more luxurious couch in the main part of the house (living room)

2006 Albuquerque—3 Weeks to Live

FEBRUARY 3, 2006
(9:00 AM MOUNTAIN TIME)

On the train to Albuquerque. Just had breakfast in the dining car. Loved it. I always love eating in the dining car while moving 80-100 miles per hour with the view of the Southwest passing by.

I sat with an Amish gentleman going to Indiana. Nice conversation—got to know him a little bit, the Amish culture and faith. Ha-he carries a Palm Treo and was talking on the darn thing like three times during breakfast! Apparently it's been getting more difficult economically for the Amish farming. With horses, I think they can farm up to about 120-180 acres.

Only about 3 ½ hours away now from Albuquerque. I like traveling by train because it puts a serious psychological distance between places, unlike air travel. It allows you to change the inner perspective.

Yesterday morning I awoke with a strange revelation. While I've done a lot of traveling and sometimes to see if a place is somewhere I'd like to live, I realized that the place I *can* and *did* live, at least momentarily was not a geographical place. It was a place in my "heart." In that place was a place where I *cared* about somebody; I cared about the good of someone. In particular, it was Becca. When I woke up, I thought the revelation was in the fact that I "lived" insider her, like finding a home. She felt very much like "home."

But as I write this, I realize home was not necessarily in Becca (which I wouldn't say no to) but a place inside my own heart; the place that was giving; the place that also received; the place that was warm, safe, and welcome. And as corny as this; as ridiculously corny as this sounds, "home is where the heart is." And when I fully felt this, I realized that I can live anywhere as long as I can live in that place in my heart where home is.

—Taking a ride over somewhere in Arizona, white sand and distant red rock cliffs are spectacular.

[illustration-amtrak window/white sand. Cows (dots). Lines are notepad lines]

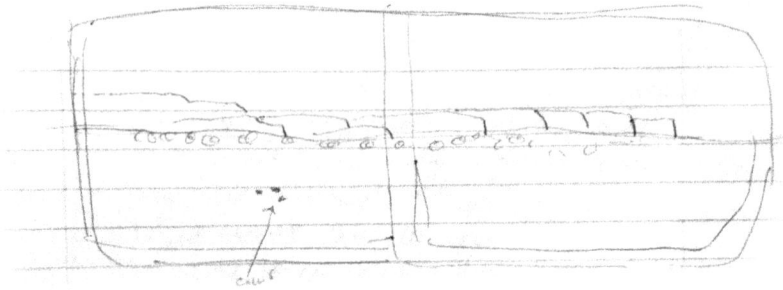

The Southwest is so amazing. The white sand looks like snow over the red.

I went out on a date yesterday and we discussed what we'd do if we only had 3 weeks to live. I thought about it for a moment and decided that I'd spend the last day alone in a natural setting such as the desert, mountain, or ocean, possibly meditating or communing with God. The remaining two weeks and 6 days would be spent meeting or seeing everyone I ever knew on Earth so far.

But what if I had a year to live? If I had a year, I'd still do those things in the last 3 weeks, plus the remaining 49 weeks would be spent traveling the world and visiting each of the Seven Wonders.

What if I had 3 years to live? Wow, that changes things. That's enough time to write a book or make a movie. So if I had 3 years, I'd make a movie in addition to the aforementioned things.

What about 5 or 10 years?

With those longer years, I thought I might live not too differently than I am now. That is to say that I'd have my goals, live my life daily, go on dates—in general, while still a good life, not as purposeful as if I had only 3 years to live.

This brings me to the idea that, first, we really don't know how much time we have here. And since that's the case, it would be wise to live in

3-year purposeful chunks. So I believe that this is what I'll do. 21 years divided by 3 is 7. I can see one of the Seven Wonders every three years. I can make one film every three years. That would be seven beautiful films. I will also spend at least one day alone in nature somewhere and reconnect with some of the people that I've met over the years.

Now this sounds great but what if we had a more optimistic view? What if not only do I live the 21 years but live for 42 more years? That changes things somewhat. What I mean by this is that the 3-year increment plan doesn't allow for something that would take 21 years to build. I know that many writers take years to write their epics. Or it might take 21 years to build a small city. Or it might take 21 years to lay rail from one part of the country to another.

In other words, if I had *that* many years and I *knew* it, I could do something that was personally meaningful. I suppose having children (and raising them) would be one of them.

It would have to be something that if I should die before 21 years, the "Project" could continue to live without me for the duration until completion or further evolvement. And should I die before then, I wouldn't feel like I failed. Somebody else could pick up the pieces and continue.

Some rules: (1) it must benefit mankind (however small) in some way. (2) Something I can do part time. (3) has a cumulative effect (each effort adds to the overall—like bricks in a building) (4) affordable (5) fairly easy to do in each increments.

Some possibilities:

Wikipedia donation (adding to the constant knowledge database)

A fine art project where a sculpture is built in a 21-year span, where (for example) brick by brick an angel or symbol of love, or symbol of home is built, perhaps to the City of Los Angeles. Can be self-funded by donors contributing bricks with an engraved name on it. Maybe near the Corn Fields. Finite number of bricks or metal patches. Somewhere near the "core" of L.A. Sculpture *should* take 21 years to build so that this symbol of home can visually, psychologically, emotionally be embedded into the hearts of the people of Los Angeles, like a tree growing. It should *not* be erected instantaneously.

I discovered my heart today. It's synonymous with home.

*Contact the woman affiliated with the Hillary Clinton Benefit.

2007 Portland

MARCH 26, 2007

(6:27 PM, MONDAY)

I didn't sleep much last night. I read over the last entry, which was just over two years ago. Two years later, here I *am*—In Portland! Honestly, I should have listened to myself and did more research for different places to live. I think Portland is "okay." The rain lives up to its reputation. The people aren't all that different until you get to that "zone." It's near Hawthrone, Belmont, Division, a good part of the inner South East which apparently thinks it represents all of Portland, if not Oregon altogether. It's a bubble of idealism, and Nazi-like politeness.

Because of time limitations in the overall scheme of things, I decided to buy a condo. While Portland is not my ideal place, it'll allow me to get a start. I hope I can last long enough for the property to appreciate and make my first feature film.

I noticed in the recent entries, there were lots of writing on relationship matters. I kind of chuckle—knowing fully the pain behind the writing and understanding. I am 40, soon to be going on 41. While I've had a few relationships, I can't say that they were very solid or even (that) meaningful. Also as I was going through the home purchasing program, I began to panic especially when we get to the point of making an offer.

I get scared thinking that my options are thoroughly limited, as if it was end of life itself. I don't quite understand it as logically it makes no sense. I think this has been a clue also as to why I may not have been in a real long-term serious relationship. Of course, the thing is when I find someone suitable, I tend to lock in—scaring the other person. Perhaps that phrase commitment-phobic applies to me. I almost (very close) dropped out of film school. It was as if the most valuable lesson in finishing my Masters was in the growth process and not necessarily in learning film.

It is time to put serious effort in changing, keeping the "follow-through" with decisions. I went to a psychiatrist before and it didn't really work years ago. But I'd like to go again with the full intent and motivation to change that. I want to have a real, loving relationship. It's been too long.

Glad I got that off my chest. I'd like to record a few events to mark this moment. On May 1st, the escrow will close on my new condo on NE68th. It's a cool, swanky place. I think I will really enjoy being there. This week also marks my 6-month anniversary of being in Portland. I am also getting a 6-month review at work: House of Antique Hardware. The work is fine as a photographer and so are the people. I could really just want a bit more money. If I don't get a decent raise, I may look for better paying work, or work in the same level but at least teach or something more flexible with my time. My current housemate is Lira Faulkner. We get along very well. The room, well, the drawing will be on the next page. I should have drawn the basement space I was in near Hawthorne, but best just to forget about that awful space.

Been dating here and there but no real success—hence the reason for seeing a therapist. I will also join a gym or do some form of exercise to get back into the swing of things. It's been over two years since the bicycle accident and I feel I could ease into it.

I will also start the writing process again in the new condo. *That* I am truly looking forward to with a view and all.

[illustration-N Dekum Street, Portland]

N. Dekum St
Portland, OR 97217
2/1/07 - 5/1/07

MAY 29, 2007

I'm now 41.

I have my new condo. Strangely, I think I bought it because in some ways of scarcity issues…NO, wait, NOT that. I meant I got it because of "Life Scarcity" issue—meaning: realizing how short (and terribly impermanent) life is, there was a part of me that wanted to do what everyone else was doing—being born, going to college, getting married, buying a home. Which brings me to why I want to be writing this journal entry. Not that doing what everyone else is doing buys you into the collective conscious, a mutual fund of consciousness of sorts. It allows and gives context to life. And by "context" I mean "meaning." It does seem to give life *some* meaning, some context, however relative or subjective. A lot of this however is driven by *fear*…sometimes total fear. We are paralyzed by this inability to think independently. And I believe this is why, perhaps, I have avoided it for so long—being married that is. At the same time, it isn't totally wrong to acknowledge the coming end—this coming end in which all or most religions are based. And in this respect, it appears Christianity is the "perfect religion." It's the religion to relieve the mind from the painful state of being alive or conscious. It is this consciousness that had been frightening most of all—because to be aware is to be totally alone, naked, and ashamed. But need it be so? Need we be frightened and ashamed? Or can we be naked, proud and unashamed? Or at least be humble and unashamed.

I had been thinking about what frightened me the most, because I felt that much of my actions were based on my fears. And when I thought about what scares me, I've come to the conclusion that it was being conscious; being alive perhaps, this unbearable consciousness. I shutter at the thought of it.

It is this *avoidance of consciousness*, both singular and collective that keeps everyone from achieving peace. Wars have been caused by this— both personal and national. Turmoil is a result of unconsciousness, or better said, ignorant of the unconsciousness, or even better said, *hiding from consciousness.*

JULY 7, 2007

Wow. Just realized today's date is "7-7-7." Well, I did get "lucky" today as one might put it. A homely Jewish girl—in a public bathroom—not something I do normally. It was just a peaceful day. A day in Tillamook at the tea house "La Tea Da."

After the "event" (the bathroom), I felt a certain sadness—though the gal was totally energized, which was good for her. For me, I felt something was lost. It was a type of spiritual realization. The sex was okay, not great, but okay. It was just that I felt the energy that was spent, the spiritual energy, was wasted.

I felt perhaps at this point, I didn't even need sex but just did it for the sake of having done it. Afterwards I wanted to connect to the other person in a much deeper way, but couldn't because I didn't feel that with her. Very, very valuable learning experience as I begin to see that my trip here to Oregon was that of spiritual growth. Today I injured myself spiritually—not just myself, but *Spirit* in general. I had done things like this before (ok, not a lot, but here and there) but…I've realized what was happening to me. I felt similar before; a bit sad, empty, and unfulfilled as before. As I see it now, I've been injuring myself many times over. I *see* it. I *see* it.

I never realized that my attempts to fulfill the emptiness were having quite the opposite effect.

I am not sad about the past. I can't really cuz I didn't know any better. But how can I now do any of what I did before, knowing what I know now?

SEPTEMBER 9, 2007

(7:08 AM)

Couple of very emotional dreams. One was that I got into Harvard University. The admissions person said it was good to go as long as one of my former instructors (or someone like that) gave the approval—and he did! (I don't know why I thought it was Paul Wunderski). I've always liked that guy.

The other dream was that my father had a stack of headshots, yes photos, of me. They were piled into a stack, turned upside down and were being cut out with a pair of scissors. I'm not sure if the images were in fact pictures of me. But in the dream that's how I identified them. Doesn't sound like a big deal, but I felt so incredibly sad, woke up physically expressing this, like bawling.

Also had images of pinecones. But that may have been right after I woke up.

[-]

Becca had visited over Labor Day weekend. It was really great to have her here. She had a crush on some guy at work which didn't work out. So I guess she needed to get away for a little while. We had a really enjoyable time visiting the Rose Garden and the Japanese Garden. We also did some hiking. We visited the idea of dating again but she said that she didn't have those feelings.

SEMPTEMBER 11, 2007

(10:31 PM, TUESDAY, HOME IN BED, IN PORTLAND OREGON)

I'm thinking of creating a Master Mind Group

SEPTEMBER 12, 2007

(5:55 AM, WEDNESDAY)

Just woke up and began to write the Master Mind group list. When I got to Don Juan about how to please a woman, he mentioned humor to make them laugh.

I realized I had the capacity for humor but some part of me didn't want to express it due to the fact that I might be laughed at or humiliated. Then I realized too that I also had negative connotations about sex, love, and money—maybe not as much with love but with sex and money and power. I want them of course and being that sex itself is a natural part of my physiology, I wonder where I got the idea that these things were *bad*. Sex and money: I know in concept that they're not bad in and of themselves, but I can't get myself to *feel* good about them. They seem somehow forbidden, as if I need permission of some sort. DJ (Don Juan) says it's a God-given right but also a gift to give—which brings me to a few other beliefs that *aren't true*: Such as "because I love filmmaking, my day job *has* to be something I don't' like." Not true.

SEPTEMBER 13, 2007

(7:38 AM, THURSDAY, IN BED)

Didn't sleep well last night. Had all those random thoughts floating around, one of which was work. Jack Eastman kept coming up. He seems very concerned about his job situation, trying to do too much. He seems paranoid. I really wish that we didn't have to work togeth-er—got that out of the way.

Mainly wanted to note that I was thinking about my 30's and I real-ize that I have made many and good efforts to do something with my life and while I don't consider it a failure, I don't feel that it was a total success either. It was a time of planting seeds and providing direction. Yet the energy spent was oftentimes wasted. Take that back. "Wasted" sounds wrong. I don't think it was until I put things down in writing that things began to take shape.

I think what's gong to help in great part is the Master Mind Group. The other is organization and *methodical* planning, much more compre-hensive.

I think the therapist's suggestion to "give yourself permission" to just write the screenplay and not look for dating was tremendously helpful. It really allows for some *clear* thought. It's not the aloneness per se, but the deliberate choice that's helping it put together.

I need to give myself permission now (there is still resistance as I write this) to enjoy (was going to say love) money, sex and power. I do. I give myself permission to be free from my old ideas about love, sex, money, and power. These things are positive things when used appro-priately.

SEPTEMBER 23, 2007

(7:23 AM, SUNDAY)

Today's the day of the big regatta.

I had a movie idea. It's inspired by the fact that I feel much love for Becca. In fact I'd like to dedicate this to her.

Basically its about a guy who's about to get married, basically engaged to this gal. they really love each other and things couldn't look rosier. Then something interesting happens. She gets an unusual form of amnesia and she doesn't remember that she's engaged to this guy—a shame because he had worked so hard to build that trust and relationship with her.

She ends up dating some other guy or maybe even guys and it's excruciatingly painful for him to see this happen. She now just sees him "just as a friend" and he has to start pursuing her again. (Note: in the beginning of the movie we find that he was always attracted to girls with certain size or shaped butt—which she has—later when she's awake and he loses his own memory, she uses this to attract him).

In any case, he stays friends with her in hopes of keeping the love alive. Like in the movie "Ladyhawk" when the characters are in their transformative state, they are *aware* of what's happening. The process takes about a day for this to happen and they are totally aware of what's happening to them. Slowly, during the course of the day (towards the third act) she begins to realize not only is this guy good for her—the truth is, she would fall in love with him again and again.

When the second transformation takes place (i.e. *he* gets amnesia) of course he drools after her. He actually forgets that he loves her and tries to sleep with her (could be a sequel). She realizes this. She knows that he will love her based on what she just experienced. She knows that he's a good person. So this frees her up to play some games with him such as teasing him in scantily clad clothing. She tortures him.

The movie ends when she realizes that the effects were caused by the food that they ate, which was caused by the water they used (from the Willamette River). Suddenly they realize there are hundreds, maybe thousands of couples who "seem" to be affected by this situation. Is it the water?

One scene that comes to mind is when our hero threatens to throw himself off the Hawthorne Bridge.

SEPTEMBER 26, 2007

(7:26 AM, THURSDAY)

The other option is to shoot Daddy's Girl as a comedy (in the spirit of Dog Day Afternoon).

Abby tortures Victoria but then says stuff like, "oh did that hurt?" She and Victoria become friends and Victoria decides to help Abby take revenge. They bitch it up.

DECEMBER 7, 2007

(7:07 AM, FRIDAY)

After many deeply sad moments (couldn't really say 'sad' so much as to say 'truthful') I wondered why I moved to Portland. I realize that not only was it not a waste, but necessary for a few reasons: (1) the mourning of my mother passing (2) [blank] (3) [blank]

But the main point that I want to write down is the fact I wish to no longer seek *meaning* and *myself*. They seem to be two things that are so worthwhile and at the same time totally useless. I mean that these two things manage to take care of themselves. To put it another way, that was *God's role.*

It makes more sense that I choose to pursue things that are: good, beautiful and funny.

While these are relative terms (i.e. relative to other people) they are absolute to the way I was designed—good, beautiful, funny.

2008 Justify—a Feature Film

MAY 2, 2008

(ABOUT 3:00 PM, FRIDAY)

It had been much too long since I'd written in here. But there's been a small inkling, a desire, to shutout the external world (which causes much pain and energy) and instead to create something small, manageable—small enough to behold, beautiful. I felt it today. But it wasn't the first time I felt this. It stems from a kind of sadness I feel; perhaps it might be called loneliness. I'm not sure.

I'm beginning to feel the need to continually create and do my work *first* and foremost, above all else, yes including doing my paying gigs. Of course I must do my paying gigs but only after having done my own *work*. I've been curious as to what makes something beautiful. Are beauty and truth synonymous? Or are the two different things? Sure, I can go look up those two words, in particular beauty. I feel I *need* beauty, especially now. I need this thing like the way I might want a glass of water when I'm thirsty. Is it possible to describe what beauty is, then go in search for this? Or is beauty, like happiness, a result or by-product of primary experience? Is "meaning" another word for beauty, thereby making a search for beauty as vain as a search for meaning?

Is beauty also a need of the mind, like meaning? Or is beauty a *primary experience* for which there is no need for explaining?

If we need to explain the beauty, is it still considered beautiful? Alibis, justifications, explanations, meanings, reasons—these are all things that beauty seems to transcend. I still don't know what it is, yet I seem to long for it as one might long for home after being in a foreign country for a while.

Are manmade objects at all beautiful? I am seeking for what seems like just a kernel of beauty, or goodness. Something is definitely happening inside. Perhaps I am looking for my "Rosebud." Are these things attainable again? If nothing short of death could bring satisfaction, I beg to wonder, this search or desire for goodness, is this an essential human need?

The word *authenticity* came to mind. What *is* beauty? How can I experience beauty? The word *essence* came to mind...*essential.* The word *sleep* comes to mind, without control.

[-]

Just took a small nap.

[-]

the word that comes to mind is *pleasure.*

JULY 20, 2008

Having not worked for about a months I'm running out of money very quickly. The thought I have this morning is about time or time management. It would seem one of the most valuable things is time, or I should say the *use* of time. Every minute should be deliberately spent, even if it means allotting time for pleasure and rest. In other words, idle time is the worst thing in the world to do. Each day should be lived—deliberately lived. Each morning, early morning before cars awake, should be spent meditating or *thinking* about the good, the beauty, or things that produce them. The most important work should be done in the morning, after meditation and exercise and before 11:00 am. Between 11-12 administrative duties (bills, phone calls) should be made. Afternoon (and after lunch) secondary work should be done. This could include errands. In the early evening before supper I should rest and relax. Also, I'm thinking from this point on I will be writing in this journal much more frequently as part of the meditative process.

Again to recap:

Wake up 5:30/6:00 AM

Meditate/Write/Exercise

Most important work, requiring *thought*

Administrative

Lunch

Secondary work/Labor

Walk

Supper

Rest

Bed by 10:00 PM

AUGUST 4, 2008

I'm going to babble on about some things. Lots going on right now with projects for potential income: iPhone software, Diamond Homes, "Justify" movie. None have immediate income but great long term prospects.

I want to review the last four feature scripts that I've written—in some ways quite ambitious. (1) Sins of the Father (2) Fat Bottom Girls (3) Justify (Daddy's Girl) (4) The Alvarado.

I think all of these have in common an attempt to grasp a theme, an idea, or philosophy. I'm beginning to think that these things are a *result* of writing about *real* situations. Instead it appears that I've been arduously plying real situations to fit these ideas. I'd like to reverse the situation for my next script. I'd like to create a real person, with real needs and wants who lives and works in a real place, a common place perhaps. It's taken one a long time to realize that no matter what I do, my "signature" or "fingerprint" will show up on all my work. In other words, my ideas and philosophies will naturally take care of themselves. On shooting "The Moment" I realize this.

So with that realization I feel quite free to explore and dig into my next script. It will be a story of love, romantic love that I've wanted to write for a while. Some ideas about it—would love for it to take place in a fishing village, or something similar. I see an old man in this some-how. I'm envisioning something in the "Il Postino" vain. But instead of Pablo Neruda, he's a fisherman—okay, I will do my best not to use the "fish in the sea" cliché. This is making me very happy already. I need to see *dirt* and *water* and *sky*. I thought about Cambria as a set-ting, or even Bodega Bay…small town.

AUGUST 5, 2008

I'm thinking there's a small child involved too. A dirty child, kind of running around in the street, a mystery child to play a key element in the story. He's wearing perhaps overalls or no shoes and has some dirt around his mouth like he ate a popsicle and the dust around him stuck to his face. When our hero tries to give him some goodies, he runs away. He appears and reappears, spying on our hero—perhaps having sex, or something. The boy is silent and doesn't say anything throughout the movie. Maybe the hero is accused of being "gay" or maybe he rapes someone. The boy is mute perhaps and sees his "friend" in court. Perhaps his friend (our hero) made him laugh inadvertently, perhaps the only one who could.

Or maybe the little boy interprets some rough sex play as rape and he somehow reports this, accuses the man of rape. And she wouldn't support the man because of class differences or race or such—that it would bring the family to ruin or shame.

AUGUST 6, 2008

(6:55 AM)

I've been waking up these days feeling drained of energy and emotional freshness. I think this has been true for quite some time. To be fully fulfilled, I think it's necessary for all body parts to *do* what they were built to do. Lately, I was thinking that my heart needed to do what it needs to do...to pump blood to the rest of the body. Aside from physical exercise, one of the ways this happens is when we are giving to others and receiving (i.e. love). Perhaps this is why the sign for love has been the heart.

Anyway as I begin to write a new script, I thought it would be interesting to write a screenplay without any death or dying. So I may modify my current notes to reflect this.

(an idea is coming to me...)

What if one of the characters is ill, perhaps depressed and decides to quit his job and take a few months off (like City Slickers) and goes away to a peaceful beautiful place, like a fishing village, or maybe wants to be a fisherman. I need this film to be a very, very positive experience, uplifting. I've been thinking a lot lately on how to change my energy from low, inverse energy (draining, sucking) to radiant, positive, life-giving energy.

As I was waking up, sunlight hit the red brick outside my bedroom window. It felt really good. I'm going to research a bit about color.

AUGUST 6, 2008

(3:22 PM)

I think it would be wise to write something that can be shot fairly inexpensively, but not have it so constricting that that is the most important thing.

ELEMENTS

-Fishing Village

-Man

-Woman

-Boy

-Old Man

-The woman's mother

-The woman's father (who was a fisherman)

-The hotel

-The Harbor/Marina

-A legend of the sea (The Sirens?)

AUGUST 7, 2008

(7:10 AM, THURSDAY)

I woke up feeling much more positive and in better mood this morning. I'm guessing a big part of it has to do with having completed the bulk of the project for Diamond Homes. Also I feel as though I will be taking on a full time job of some sort. I also feel I will make another short, something *really, really, really* good to win at major film festivals.

Clarity and direction: I'm not sure whether Justify will be made soon honestly. But I still feel I'm on the right track. The story should have a unique setting or situation, something people generally aren't familiar with; something that happens all the time or people we are familiar with but don't' talk about for whatever reason.

I'm beginning to see that "cleanliness" (being free of clutter and stress) is making me feel good.

AUGUST 8, 2008

Some thoughts for the new script: I need to come up with a situation, a predicament. One thought is to use Abby and Victoria's situation and finish the story that way. For example, we can start with Abby's wounded (choose your favorite bleeding body part) leg and have them driving into the night trying to find a hospital with an emergency room that will take them in—a public clinic and waiting for hours to get help. In the meantime we know that they're running from the law and still must deal with the newfound relationship of mother/sister. That's certainly one idea and I think a pretty good one. I love the idea of the "what ifs." Revisiting what I wrote the last few days, I will incorporate the characters and situations from there...from "elements."

AUGUST 27, 2008

(7:30 AM)

"You don't have to yell at a rose for it to bloom."

I have a freelance photography gig today. The main reason for the entry was the dream I had last night. Both mom and dad were in it. The feelings were quite strong so I needed to write them down. Dad was found renovating an old home. In fact, he was putting in gorgeous new stain glass windows (or something similar)—very large I might add. He seems happy. He was the only one there besides me.

The other part of the dream consisted of meeting Cynthia Beethoven where my mother lives. Apparently, she lives many miles away, south along this road or trail. I had to tread through mud to get there. Only when I got there, it wasn't it. I asked someone for directions, I was told that it was an additional 16 miles (south as I understand it).

Too far to continue walking, I started hitchhiking. Suddenly I was doing this in what appears to be the Great Depression. Men were riding along in cramped old trucks with wood rails along this small road near a town.

I don't know why Cynthia came into my dream or why I was supposed to meet her where my mother is, but that's what I was doing. I woke up before I got there. There were no bad feelings about any part of the dream. Other than the lack of color, everything was in that grey muddy color. In fact muddy trails were the norm. It felt "normal" or even positive.

I think Cynthia was there because I wrote her an honest email about her not showing up and calling thereafter for "forgiveness." I said that she was trying to save face, not really looking for forgiveness.

AUGUST 29, 2008

(12:35 AM, TECHNICALLY STILL THURSDAY NIGHT)

Just had an idea for a short—about a dying grandmother or grandfather and the family's reunion to see her for the last time. ~~Grandma has a wish. Grandma is on her last few breaths.~~

OCTOBER 13, 2008

ITVS Story idea.

About a kooky old guy who frequently visits the post office. He's old, perhaps only 70's. At the post office, he picks up his social security check. He picks up supplies from the post office, supplies he uses to make strange little baby toys that he sells. Some he keeps. He's got a bit of a drinking problem ever since his wife had left him for a career. He uses an online auction to sell some of these things. But mostly he keeps these things for himself and has them all over his house.

His wife apparently didn't want to have a child and he thought eventually she would change his mind. She didn't. He used to donate sperm when young for extra money and fun.

One day he walks into the post office when he collapses

[story not completed]

2009 - 2010 Post Production

[Editing my first feature film "Justify"]

2011 Energy

JULY 1, 2011

(8:36 AM FRIDAY)

It has been a very long time since I've written in here. But it's significant enough that I do so. I've been having less of those "waking up sad" feelings lately, probably since I'd last written. Anyway the last few days, week, or so I've been feeling the sadness again. But this time, I finally know why (or at least have something to attribute it to). The sadness comes from a disconnect in relationships with people. The giving and receiving of love (or even other feelings such as anger) has been absent or severed. In some ways this is not a bad thing because it seems it would be better to be empty; to be with potential; to be (potentially) filled with good feelings and ideas—rather than destructive ones.

It's the *first time* I'm realizing this in my consciousness.

This relates to my curiosity lately concerning energy—how everything in the universe including my body is essentially energy: exchanging, transforming, growing, and decaying.

I'm very curious about how energy works. From the macro to the micro, we are balls of energy. Money, environment, love, athletics—all are energy. It seems *all* of my problems (and perhaps the world's and the universe's) are matters of energy. Do we waste? Do we hoard?

The way people utilize energy keeps them wealthy or poor. What is energy? Is there a purpose for it? What does energy want to do?

Certain words come to mind: Intention—Wayne Dyer. Thoughts are things—Napoleon Hill. Consciousness/Matter—Matter being possibly a *result* of consciousness. Is energy a form of consciousness?

Or perhaps energy IS consciousness.

Things like dishonesty is essentially misdirection in the use of energy and can only be destructive to the flow of energy.

The language of Energy is the same as the money metaphor (currency). Money itself is a measure of energy, either measured my manpower or "thought currency" and then represented by the numeric symbols put onto paper.

The question becomes, how do we control the source of energy within that affects all energy without?

It seems all energy passes through certain range of frequencies or vibrations.

The human emotion (energy in motion), I believe is a ball of energy that controls *everything*. As in Napoleon Hill's book [*Think and Grow Rich*], infuse that energy (emotion) with thoughts (carrier signals—my words) and that should give you the steering wheel to *everything*.

www.ingramcontent.com/pod-product-compliance
Lightning Source LLC
LaVergne TN
LVHW011348080426
835511LV00005B/190